⊛OUTSIDE LOOKING IN

High-functioning autism from one mother's perspective

OUTSIDE LOOKING IN

High-functioning autism from one mother's perspective

by

Vivian M. Lumbard

TABLE OF CONTENTS

INTRODUCTION

If you are reading this book, then you probably want to further your understanding of Autism Spectrum Disorder (ASD). Perhaps someone you love is autistic (and that someone could be yourself) or you are a special needs professional. Or maybe you are an educator in a general classroom environment seeing more autistic children in your classes. No matter your reason for choosing this book, I sincerely hope that our family's story adds value to your life in some positive way.

A fair warning: While I am the closest thing there is to an expert on my children—a daughter who has high-functioning autism and a son who would most likely be diagnosed as autistic if he shared his sister's social awareness issues—I am far from any sort of psychological or neurological expert overall, and I don't have all the answers you may be seeking. There are days when I'm not even sure I understand the questions. Each family's journey with autism is as unique as a fingerprint.

Not every situation I share within this book specifically deals with autism. I thought it would be helpful for you to have some background and insight on me and my husband, John, as individuals and parents, as it has affected our choices for our children. But I'll start you off with a little information here. I have a Type AAA personality, while John would qualify as Type ZZZ. I grew up in what could be called a volatile, dysfunctional family in suburban Massachusetts, while John was raised in a stable, loving family in Pittsburgh. John is an excavator with his own business, and I'm a retired air traffic controller who spent a great deal of time as a union activist. I like to have an overall plan of action (like a consistent bedtime routine for the kids), but John is far more relaxed.

How we have chosen to handle the challenges of living with autism directly stems from who we are and how we parent. Taking into consideration the rapid pace of today's society, John and I consciously elected to let our children experience the magic of childhood for as long as possible and not to force them to leave it before they naturally did so on their own. If that meant they believed in the Easter Bunny for a couple of extra years, then that was alright. We have chosen carefully worded honesty over bluntness or avoidance and allowed the children to lead their own journeys towards maturity with us making course corrections along the way.

You see, long before we knew we were living with autism, John and I believed we were parenting two unique children who we wanted to grow into the best versions of themselves. The knowledge of autism in our lives did not change that belief; it only reinforced it. We are simply parenting two complex individuals whom we love dearly.

From the time I learned I was pregnant until our children started school, I kept a journal for each of them. My thought process was that John and I were older parents and life itself was uncertain. I wanted to ensure that our children had something tangible to remind themselves of how much I loved them should I not be there for them in the future. Once school started, I couldn't find time to keep up with the journals. Then, when I began writing this book, it was originally for our children, so that they could have a glimpse into why their parents made the choices they did. Hopefully they would realize that we understood them better than they might currently believe as they traverse their teen years. Somewhere along the line, I began to believe that the story of our journey thus far might benefit others.

Our family life is far richer than just living with autism. Yours should be too. Take the time to enjoy each other in between the tougher times. Everything we do stems from our love for each member of our family.

A note on terminology: Some people prefer *autism*; others prefer *autistic*. I have no preference and use the words simply as a noun or adjective respectively. I believe the phrase *living with autism* is far more accurate for all members of the family, even if it is a little more cumbersome at times. The word *neurotypical* is used as a noun and adjective meaning not having ASD. I use the word *meltdown* to describe the outburst or breakdown of self-control autistic people experience and exhibit when they have difficulty coping.

I've been asked by early readers of this book what the title, *Outside Looking In*, signifies. Many times, I have had the impression that our daughter feels as if she is outside looking in at the neurotypical community and behaviors. I know I have felt as if I am outside looking in at her autistic world. And now you are outside looking in at our family's journey.

The experiences I have written about are true. I asked our children to review my first draft of this book to determine if there was anything I may have shared that would make them uncomfortable so that I could remove it. John and I were gratified to see them approach potentially embarrassing sections with the mindset of "It happened a long time ago," or "Every parent tells these types of stories about their kids," and my personal favorite, "Will this help someone else with autism?"

However, most names have been changed. Not because of any shame or embarrassment, but because our twins have just turned fifteen and their privacy is important to me. Also, our daughter does not yet have the self-confidence to publicly own all her autistic trials for the entire world to see. I do not feel I have the right to make that irreversible decision for her.

Our daughter has one of the starring roles in our lives, and I hope the day comes, sooner rather later, when she will feel comfortable claiming that role in this book, if only to her closest friends. My fervent wish is that someday she sees herself as her dad and I see her: as an incredibly creative, intelligent, funny, loving, strong young lady growing into a wonderful woman.

Baby girl, we are so amazed by you every single day. You are so much more capable than you give yourself credit for, and our pride in you has no bounds.

And to our dear sweet boy, your unfettered joy in life and your desire to share that joy as well as your unwavering love, support, and understanding of your sister make us immensely proud to be your parents.

To everyone else in our village of people who have lent or are still lending aid along our journey, whether it is a shoulder to cry on, a bracing hand, a supportive push, or pulling us along when we are tired, thank you for everything—especially your love and care of our children when they are with you, learning and growing.

CHAPTER 1

IMAGINE

"Once upon a time, in a land not so far away…"
That's how my mom always begins her social stories.

THE WORDS ABOVE are ones I imagine my children might say if the subject ever came up. I've used variants of social stories with our twins, not realizing there was a name for them, long before we had a diagnosis. If you don't work or live with someone with autism, you might need an explanation. A *social story* is a short story, many times individualized, used to depict a situation, skill, or concept with social cues and appropriate or common responses. They are designed to assist someone with Autism Spectrum Disorder (ASD) in gaining better understanding of what is expected of them by the neurotypical community. The social story that follows will hopefully help you gain a better understanding of what is experienced by those with autism.

Imagine, if you will, that you're headed out for a night out at the hottest club in town. You are wearing new clothes that look great but may be just a little bit uncomfortable with a seam that is a bit too wide somewhere and letting itself be known occasionally as you move around. The venue is packed with people, and it seems everyone overdid it on the perfume and cologne. It is hot. People are sweaty, and you can smell spilled alcohol. Every once in a while, you get a whiff of the sweetness of the fruit garnishments used in the drinks. The place is huge with high ceilings, and it is loud. The owners of the club decided to maximize their establishment's appeal by dividing the building into quarters, each playing a different type of music; some live, some with a DJ. Near the center of the room, you can hear all of them jumbled together.

You pick a place to stand with your friends and have a drink or two. Although all of you keep trying, talking is next to impossible with the noise. The strobe lights exaggerate people's expressions as they talk and their body language as they move. It becomes almost painful to look at your companions and try to determine what is being said.

You realize you've forgotten to have dinner when you reach for your drink and your hand doesn't quite go where you think you are telling it to go. Everything is just a little off, but you decide to head to the nearest dance floor and dance it off. Between the alcohol and the lighting, your movements feel uncoordinated and jerky, and sometimes you think you may fall. You close your eyes and it appears better for a bit, but now the odors and sounds seem more prominent to your senses. Your head starts to ache and even your skin starts to get a creepy-crawly feeling.

Finally, it all becomes too much and you decide to grab a car service home. Maybe you drink some water and pop a couple aspirin before heading to bed, planning a nice hot shower in the morning. Previous experience tells you that you should feel normal about noon the next day, at which time you will have a better idea of when you may decide to head to the club again. But why would you want to go again?

Even though the end result of the evening was fatigue, maybe some irritation, and a general sense of not feeling right, there were aspects that you really enjoyed. Maybe it was the crush of the bodies creating a sense of security as you waited at the bar for a drink, the rush of the air around your body as you danced and spun creating a sense of freedom, or the thrumming of the bass deep in your bones as you stood near one of the speakers creating echoes throughout your body. Whatever it was, there were parts of the evening when your body felt absolutely wonderful.

The sensory overload of your night on the town is something autistic people live with every single day. The degree to which it affects their ability to cope with it is dependent on many factors. What successful coping strategies they've learned, their age, the supports they have in place, what senses get overloaded and by how much, what stressors are involved, how much sleep they had the night before, and even whether they're coming down with a cold are only some of the factors that come into play. Obviously, neurotypical individuals experience sensory overload too. For me, there is a large flea market less than an hour from our home we occasionally visit that is guaranteed to send me over the edge. There is one section inside where a seller has boxes on shelves and the floor covered with items jumbled together with absolutely no sense of order—I mean, silverware in the same box with dolls and tools? By the time we meander there and I see that stall, the visual overload is too overwhelming for me; I have to get out immediately. I go from having a good time searching for treasures to absolute crankiness instantly.

Ever gotten irritable on a hot, steamy day? Or from being around crowds of people at a parade? Overwhelmed by the scents in the laundry aisle at the grocery store? There may be other issues involved too, but sensory overload is likely a big part of it. The difference is, as neurotypicals, the vast majority of time, we can choose to remove ourselves from a sensory-overload situation. Those with autism cannot. They can learn to cope, but they, just like us, are not always successful. They do not choose to have a meltdown when it becomes too much. They simply have no choice and are trying to cope in the best way they can.

You may ask, "Why can't they just tell us so we can help them?" To answer that, we have to go back to the nightclub scenario. If you are neurotypical, you understand the resting point of "normal" and you probably intuitively understood from the description that your senses just had too much input on too many fronts at once. You and I have a common frame of reference for both parts of the equation. But those on the spectrum, especially children, do not have that common experience of normal sensory input; they have no way to explain what causes the difference because they do not understand the resting point—they have never experienced it. It would be like expecting a person blind from birth to explain what the color blue looks like, or a person born deaf to explain how shrill sounds. The autistic normal *is* too much sensory input. On the other hand, there are occasions when they receive too little sensory input. Remember why you wanted to go back to the nightclub? Regardless, they do not have the luxury of knowing what neurotypical people consider normal.

Once they gain proficiency managing the sensory input and begin to be aware of their own individual resting points, many autistic people are able to explain what sensory inputs cause them distress and can expound on both sides of their own equation. However, I'm not sure that it has ever been proven or disproven that their individual resting points are similar to those of neurotypical people. As such, the autistic individual can only compare to what he/she considers normal, which may not necessarily be the same for a neurotypical person.

You have probably heard of the ongoing campaign for autism awareness. There is some debate that the focus of the campaign should shift to autism acceptance. Personally, I believe we should aim for autism understanding. I also believe that with the growing numbers of children diagnosed with autism, that understanding is getting exponentially closer. Many more families now have the knowledge that they are living with autism, while more educators are receiving training and experience with autistic students. More and more people with ASD are sharing their perceptions and stories.

But the key is the families, the siblings that grow up with and love their brothers and sisters with autism. Those siblings may not understand all the ins and outs of autism, but they understand the potential triggers and stressors and coping strategies. Most importantly of all, they understand that their sibling is a much more complex individual beyond some arbitrary label. And in the not-so-distant future, those siblings are the ones who will be best able to recognize people on the spectrum and not only accept them, but also compassionately understand them, as the whole unique individuals that they are.

CHAPTER 2

I KNEW YOU BEFORE
YOU WERE BORN

Once when young,
I dreamed of a girl and a boy
Arriving together
Filling my days with light and joy...

FROM THE TIME I was seven years old, I knew I was going to have boy/girl twins the first time I became pregnant. I intuited that fact deep in my bones and never once questioned the knowledge. While a few close friends knew about my premonition over the years, I didn't advertise it far and wide. Why have people think you're out of your mind when you don't have to, right?

I became interested in genealogy in my early twenties and discovered that twins do run on one side of my family, but not every other generation as is typical. In my case, it had been the oldest child of the oldest child every third generation all the way back to 1640, and I was the next in line. Confirmation?

If nothing else, that knowledge was an effective means of birth control for many years, until I felt I was emotionally and financially ready (oh yeah, I discovered you are never truly financially ready!) for children. When my relationship with John had progressed to the point of discussions of our future, I let him in on the knowledge. He claims to have believed me; I think he was willing to humor me.

Anyway, John had children from a previous marriage, and I wanted him to be sure about the decision to have children together, since I knew we were going to have twins if we did. We tried for a year. Nothing. We got tested. Other than a small percentage of funky-shaped sperm on his end, there was no obvious reason why we hadn't been successful. Another few months went by, and I sat my husband down for a serious talk in January 2004. I told him I couldn't be one of those women who cried every month; I needed an end date where we stopped pinning our hopes on Mother Nature and would begin the adoption process instead. We decided that if we weren't pregnant by the end of the summer, we would adopt.

Lo and behold, Mother's Day 2004, my little pregnancy test read: POSITIVE. Yeah! It's still one of my favorite Mother's Days. I think I just needed the pressure about conceiving off my mind before my body would decide to cooperate. About a month later, I started saying "they" whenever I talked of my pregnancy. Both John and my best friend, Karen (Auntie Karen to our children), tried to dissuade me, saying they did not want me disappointed if I was incorrect. Blithely, I assured them I wasn't wrong. A month after that, I told John that his son was on my right side and his daughter on my left.

At my twenty-week appointment, I talked briefly with my doctor about the birthing plan I had developed. He suggested that I just tell the medical staff what I wanted when I was in labor, since his experience had been that only one person a year came to him with a birthing plan, and it never went according to plan. He was right; only one item on the plan happened the way I wanted it. But all the research I had done beforehand gave me much-needed insight into the causes affecting the doctor's decisions during my labor.

I told the doctor I was pretty sure I was having twins. Mind you, until this point, we had only heard one heartbeat. Even though I was thirty-nine years old and overweight, my pregnancy had been going very smoothly. (Well, except for morning sickness in my second trimester, which was so not fair.) Doc just said, "Wouldn't that be cool?" and reminded me that my first ultrasound appointment was the next day.

Tomorrow arrived and I told the ultrasound technician that I was certain there were two babies in there. She said, "We'll know in a moment," placed the wand on my stomach, and said, "Yep, there are two babies." She did what she needed to do for Baby A, our son, Beckett, and instructed me take a bathroom break. (Yeah!) When I got back, I asked John, "Are you ready to meet your daughter?" His smart-aleck reply: "Oh, you're so sure it's a girl?" My response was "Have I been wrong yet?" We then got to see our daughter, April, otherwise known as Baby B, for the first time. Oh, and they were both exactly where I had told John they would be.

There was another physician in my regular doctor's office who wanted me to go on bedrest at twenty-four weeks for no reason other than I was having twins. Despite that, the other doctors expected me to go to full-term (forty weeks), as if I was having a singleton… right up until the day before I was thirty-five weeks. On that fateful day, the medical professionals didn't like the readings they were receiving on April during the non-stress test. My children never wanted to cooperate with these tests, which were conducted twice a week, but this time, I was sent directly from that hospital to a neo-natal specialist at a Pittsburgh hospital for more tests. Long story short, April's amniotic fluid had dropped suddenly, and they induced me the next day.

While they are really good stories, I won't bore you with all the tales between the time I called John to finish packing my hospital bag and the delivery. Suffice it to say, I pushed the two of them out eventually. Beckett had tachypnea, which is abnormally rapid breathing, and was whisked away to the neonatal intensive care unit (NICU) before I could see him. They did not let me meet my firstborn in person until six hours later, but I was able to see my beautiful girl in my husband's arms before she was taken to the regular nursery.

The next night at about three o'clock, two nurses brought a screaming April to my room. They apologized for waking me, since they knew I needed my rest after having delivered twins, but they had tried everything and just could not calm her. I took her, saying, "She's my daughter; of course you can wake me." As soon as she was in my arms, she stopped crying. The nurses looked at each other and laughed, saying, "She obviously knows what she wants, and she wants Mommy."

I was discharged from the hospital within two days, but I was lucky enough to be able to nest at the hospital (they allowed me to stay in an empty room at no additional cost after I was discharged) until both children were ready to come home. April was in the regular nursery for six days; Beckett was in NICU, then was stepped down and discharged in seven days. Early on in that week, I'd had a meltdown when they put Beckett under bili lights without telling me. I read the nurse's notes later, which said something to the effect that I was very emotional but that as soon as I was able to hold my son, I was fine. I had had lots of prior experience with babies and children, and I had conducted an enormous amount of research on what to expect during labor and childbirth. But I had had no experience or real knowledge of the part between birth and going home. With no access to a library or the internet, I was feeling lost and unprepared. I absolutely detested being uninformed, and **these were my babies**. I may have overreacted, but the hospital assigned someone specifically to keep me in the loop of any changes in medical care to my children—which really was in everyone's best interests.

At the time, we also owned a snow-removal business. John enjoys telling the story of how he took the family snowplowing on the way home from the hospital. The kids find the story amusing. Me, I was just glad that we were all out of the hospital, together as a family.

Beckett and April love to hear these stories. They love knowing that I knew them before they were even conceived.

CHAPTER 3

THE EARLY YEARS

Morning, noon, night
The beginning of firsts.
Warm hugs, eyes bright;
Each day, the wonder of new.

BEFORE I GET into our lives, there is something I should probably share about myself. Many people who knew me prior to my becoming a mom would characterize me as a tough woman who never cried. I have survived various traumas, thrived in spite of it all, and I was a woman in a male-dominated profession. While I did have some weepy moments while childless, it was rare that anyone outside my close circle would see my tears.

When the pressures of life built up, and I knew I needed the release, I would occasionally plan a weekend to be depressed and miserable all by myself. I'd stay in my pajamas, eat comfort foods, watch tear-jerker movies, and weep anywhere and anytime the urge hit. At the end of the weekend, I would put on my big-girl panties, and Ms. Can-Handle-Anything ventured back out into the big, bad world. The thought of crying in front of others, or even admitting I needed to cry, was abhorrent to me.

After giving birth, that changed. My emotions were much closer to the surface. I no longer cared whether anyone saw me tear up and reach for a tissue. Maybe it's having twenty people in your delivery room in one of your most exposed moments, maybe it's just mom hormones or a combination of both, but I didn't even try to hold back tears anymore.

≈

I took leave from my job as an air traffic controller for almost four months before going back part-time for a month, then returning to full-time status. My commute was over an hour long each way in good weather and traffic. I also worked rotating shifts and rotating days off. John went part-time around my schedule since we had decided that we wanted to be the primary caregivers for our children. We were fortunate that we had the ability to make it all happen.

It was a busy time. Twins are wonderful, but a lot of work. People ask me how I handled it, and all I can say is you just do it because you have to—no different from any other parent. Beckett and April have been each other's best friend ever since they were wombmates. They also are each other's partner in crime. John and I used to joke that by age twenty-five, they would either have won the Nobel Peace Prize or be on the FBI's Most Wanted List as mastermind criminals.

The following paragraphs are just snapshots of their early years, and at first glance, it might seem as if I was the perfect, patient, understanding supermom. While I would love to claim that unachievable moniker, the reality was that sometimes I would get so tired and overwhelmed that I would lock myself in the bathroom just for a few moments of peace or to calm myself. I pushed my mental and physical resources to the limits and frequently misjudged how much I could realistically handle.

When I was losing patience with their misbehavior, it wasn't unusual for the children to hear me counting out loud in a very slow, deliberate tone. When they were toddlers, we began teaching the children to breathe deep into their bellies when they were distressed or crying: in through the nose and out through the mouth. But sometimes I still yelled much louder or longer than necessary. I broke a window pane in one of our French doors on two separate occasions by slamming the door in anger. I still count and yell, just not nearly as often since I retired, but it has been many, many years since I've broken that door.

General

We used to call April our old soul because her eyes looked like they had already seen a lifetime's worth of experiences. She would watch people for a long time before deciding whether or not she wanted to interact with them.

Beckett was our power-puker and a social butterfly who felt things—body, mind, and soul. It was depressing to work so hard to produce enough milk for the two of them and then have him regurgitate it to a distance of six to eight feet away. The kid has also never met a stranger, which can be terrifying for a parent. I have a niggling mom worry that someday someone is going to break his wonderful heart and crush his spirit.

When they were about six months old, I came home to an excited John wanting to show me what he had taught the kids. He handed them their bottles, and they sloppily fed themselves. This was an eye-opening, dope-slap moment for me. I had been so busy trying to keep pace with the never-ending, rolling to-do list in my head that it had never occurred to me to slow down and just take the time to let the children learn how to do it on their own. My flexible, Gumby-ish, willing-to-clean-up-the-inevitable-messes husband taught me more than he taught our children that day.

When they were old enough, we discussed "good secrets" and "bad secrets." Good secrets were those that would cause other people happiness, like a surprise birthday party, or the kinds friends share. Bad secrets were those that involved someone getting hurt or thinking about hurting themselves or others. We told them that sometimes people do things that hurt someone and then tell that person that they would hurt someone else if he/she told the secret. These were the most dangerous bad secrets, and it was important they told them to us. John and I let them know that we expected them to keep good secrets, because that is what good friends do, but bad secrets—no matter how scary—had to be shared with us so that we could make sure everyone stayed as safe as possible.

When they were toddlers, there were times when I would work a day shift, then quick turn to a midnight shift, which in air traffic control we shortened to *midshift*. Then I would have to care for our children during the day so John could go to work. Sometimes the exhaustion would be too much for me, and I would move all of us to a room—what we called our library—and after the children ate, I'd make sure there were plenty of things to keep them busy, close the door, lay down in front of it, and take a nap. The only way out for them was to try to crawl over my sleeping body. Not a perfect solution, by any means, but I would guess that most parents have done something similar when necessary. Some days, you do what you have to in order to keep them safe and still survive yourself.

If I tried to put barrettes in April's hair, she would pull them out immediately. She once let me put her hair in ponytails for a Special Olympics event, and our hairdresser was able to convince her to try "Indian princess braids" one day. Other than that, she has never let me do anything with her hair.

For many years, April would not speak on the phone. She would listen intently, nod, and shake her head, but would not speak. Eventually, she would say a few words to me when I called from work or travel. Even today, she is more likely to text than call, although I have heard her on the phone with friends as they played video games. Beckett, on the other hand, has always loved to talk on the phone.

Health

I've never been one of those panicky moms. Maybe it was all those previous years of babysitting; maybe it was being an older mom; maybe it's just my personality or some combination of all three reasons. Before he retired, our pediatrician would talk about me walking in with two babies in infant car seats for appointments each time we saw each other. When the kids were about two and a half months old, I took them in for their first sick visit. I told him I was hoping I was just being an overprotective mom, but I really didn't like the way they sounded. After they had been checked out, the plan of action was two different treatments with a nebulizer (one every four hours, the other every six) and an antibiotic (every eight hours). If they weren't better in twenty-four hours, the doctor was going to hospitalize them for bronchitis because they were so young. The pharmacy filled the prescriptions while I was still at the pediatrician's office being taught how to give the nebulizer treatments. I picked up the prescriptions and went home to make a chart, factoring in how long each nebulizer treatment took, so I knew what to do with which child when. Oh, have I mentioned that there was a snowstorm and John was out plowing? I was on my own for this.

The next day, car seats filled and babies in hand, I returned bug-eyed to the doctor's office. "Mommy did her homework; they sound much better." I hopefully asked if we could give up one of the treatments in the middle of the night so I could get some sleep. Luckily, he agreed, as long as they sounded alright at bedtime. Whew!

John came home after being out about thirty-six hours. I showed him the schedule and how to do the treatments, saying, "I know you're tired, but I need two hours sleep or I'm going to collapse." He let me sleep three hours before he hit his own max-critical wall. That's one of the best traits my husband possesses. When it is truly necessary, he always does his best to come through for us. I just have to let him know what it is we need.

April became colicky late and stayed that way later than most; she started at about nine weeks and continued past four months. Luckily for us, she only needed to be held constantly; it didn't matter who it was. Just as luckily, Beckett was happy in his infant seat with me holding his sister, so long as I would verbally interact with him. I remember one day, both kids were incessantly crying for what seemed like hours. I called John and desperately asked how long it would be before he came home because I needed another set of hands—five minutes ago. He was only ten minutes from home, so my sanity was saved that day. It still amazes me that some days could feel so interminably long, yet the years flew by.

At some point, it changed, and Beckett became our cuddle bug, while April did not want to be held at all. I tearfully told my friend Karen that I was worried that April would grow up thinking we didn't want to hold her or love her as much as her brother when all we were doing was respecting her wishes. Karen talked me down from that hormonal mom ledge, and two days later, April wanted to cuddle again like her brother.

While our children have been amazingly healthy overall, there still were occasions when fevers, colds, and ear infections visited our home. April also had a bout of Fifth Disease, which sounds far worse than it actually is—it's just a rash.

When they were toddlers, giving April medicine was a battle for a long time. She would immediately gag and spit it out. I tried mixing the medicine with food or drinks, but would have no success. I remember eventually having to restrain her by almost sitting on her to keep her still enough to pinch her nose closed and insert the plastic syringe into her mouth far enough that she would have no choice but to swallow. Both of us would be in tears each and every time, until she was able to handle ingesting her medicine without gagging. I hated having to give her medicine that way, but I couldn't find any other option that would work to get her healthy or pain-free again.

⤎

Sometimes it felt as if my optometrist was a sister from another mother. She was also from the East Coast, had relocated to our area, had boy/girl twins a few years older than ours, held a similar outlook on life, and had a sense of humor compatible with mine.

When the children were about eleven months old, I had an annual eye exam. We talked about our respective children, and she asked me to bring Beckett and April in with me for my contact lenses check so she could meet them. I did, and she decided to briefly check the children's eyes at no charge. Afterwards, she suggested that I have them seen by the pediatric specialist in her office for a more thorough exam.

Of course, I made the appointment, and we discovered that Beckett had hyperopia— farsightedness. His high degree of hyperopia meant he required glasses to keep one eye from crossing. While Beckett was very good about wearing his glasses, he was a toddler and he broke them regularly. One year, we were replacing his glasses every two months. It was a long time before he was able to go a full year without some kind of mishap.

⤎

One year, just after Easter, I was sitting in the living room and heard choking noises from Beckett, who was standing at the window. I jumped off the couch to find that he had put one half of a large plastic Easter egg in his mouth with the pointy end pointing towards his throat. It had created a seal that wasn't letting him breathe. I couldn't get it out immediately, tried patting his back, and performed a mini-Heimlich maneuver, all the while watching him start to turn blue. I was finally able to insert a finger between his inner cheek and the egg to break the seal and remove the offending item. It probably wasn't more than several seconds, but it felt like a terribly long lifetime to me. A few minutes later, John came home to Beckett and me rocking together, crying uncontrollably. I tearfully instructed John to find every plastic Easter egg in the house and throw them away. Over a decade later, those toys are still not allowed in our house and never will be. I am exceedingly grateful that I was in the room when it happened; imagining otherwise kept me up more than a few nights afterwards.

It took us years before we were successful in convincing April to even sit in the dentist's chair to have her teeth looked at, let alone cleaned. I think Beckett had already had four semi-annual cleanings before she had one.

Before they started pre-K, we took April to a foot specialist, as she suffered from overpronation, which resulted in her wearing plastic braces for about a year. She doesn't remember wearing them, but she was very good about them.

Neither child was walking by fifteen months, and our pediatrician asked if we wanted to have them tested. Neither John nor I were worried since they were concentrating on other skills, including finding programs on my computer that I didn't even know existed, so we didn't do so. Beckett was walking the next day. He still tiptoes regularly and has calves of iron. April walked three months later.

I sometimes wonder, if we had had them tested then, would we have done things differently? In some ways, I think our ignorance and innate parenting style of understanding our children's personalities and adjusting our interactions to best support them worked to our advantage. As far as we were concerned, they were just learning and growing in their own ways. They still are.

Diet

I made almost all Beckett and April's baby food. I would cook, steam, boil, puree, and freeze. The only food they didn't like was asparagus, and I have the pictures to prove it. My thought process was that we could expose them to all different kinds of food and bypass the picky-eater stage. They weren't even allowed a French fry until they were eighteen months old. Unfortunately, it didn't work. We now have two of the pickiest eaters on the face of the planet, and it doesn't seem to be changing any time soon. I think it might be partially sensory based, but it is still frustrating. I worry that they might not getting the range of nutrients that their bodies require to stay healthy.

April loved buffalo chicken dip; she must have been the one who wanted hot wings twice a week during my pregnancy. We would find her sitting on the kitchen floor, spoon in hand, cheerfully eating cold, congealed leftover dip from the open refrigerator. We could not keep her out of the refrigerator, even if there was no dip to be had, and ended up locking the appliance for years.

Gross Motor Skills

Beckett was a climber from about eight months on. One day, I watched him pull a big, cube-shaped stuffed toy over to an end table next to a buffet chest in front of the dining room window. He then pulled a chair over to the other side of the chest. Crawling over to the stuffed cube toy, he climbed up onto it, then onto the end table, and finally onto the chest to look out the window. When he was finished, he climbed down onto the chair and back down to the floor. I relayed the story to John saying, "He was planning his exit strategy before he even started. We are in so much trouble."

Another time, Beckett was attempting to go down headfirst from our high pillowtop mattress. I would stop him each time, turning him around saying, "Always feet first." John watched us for a while before finally saying, "You know he's still going to fall, right?" I just replied, "Yes, but at least he'll fall on his bottom or maybe hit the back of his head, not break his neck. We can't stop him from climbing, but we can minimize his chances of getting seriously hurt."

April never really crawled but instead scooted on her back and used to arch her back and neck in odd ways. Man, was she fast! Poor kid had a bald patch on the back of her head until she started walking.

᠊ᡃᢙ᠊

Fine Motor Skills

When John and I were first teaching the children how to write their letters and numbers, it was an extremely painful process for Beckett, and by extension, us. He would get frustrated and scream whenever whatever he had written didn't look like what he had had in mind. But when he wrote it the way he had envisioned, he would hold the paper in both hands, shake it happily with a big grin, and make a gleeful noise. Sometimes, he would run around and flap his hands. He still does both, and only when he's excited; it's like there is so much happiness and joy in his body that he just has to let it out or explode. Later, during his school years, teachers would contact us about his self-stimulation behavior (more commonly referred to as a *stim*), but we have never been concerned about it.

April, on the other hand, had and still has chicken-scratch handwriting. She actually dislikes the physical act of writing letters and holds writing implements in an odd way. Graphology is sometimes called brain-writing. Perhaps her handwriting is an indicator of how her brain works differently than a neurotypical brain. I find it interesting, though, that as a baby, she would easily pick up tiny pieces of lint from the carpet.

Early on, Beckett became very interested in drawing, first on a DoodlePro, then on paper. He was quite prolific; I was buying three cases of paper at a time to keep up with him. He could often be found running around the house with a fistful of loose sheets, stopping wherever inspiration hit him, drawing whatever was in his head and then doing his happy stim. We tried unsuccessfully for years to get him to use a sketchbook, even though it would have been more expensive, in an attempt to contain the paper mess in our home.

When we visited the pediatrician's office, both children would draw on the paper that covered the examination table. I think their doctors enjoyed seeing the pictures, and I know I enjoyed that the children were able to keep themselves quietly occupied while waiting.

Transitions & Literal Language

When he was old enough, Beckett became obsessed with schedules and time. If we'd said we were going to leave at 10:00, he was upset by 10:02 if we hadn't gotten out the door. He was, and still is, very literal. It took us years to get him to understand good-natured teasing. With his current interest in puns, his wordplay skills have improved.

On the other hand, April has long been quite capable of understanding metaphor and wordplay. Her vocabulary has always been worlds above her peers. Seriously, what nine-year-old uses the words *peckish* and *vambrace* in normal conversation, let alone correctly? She was a constant chatterbox—acting out scenes from movies, making up pretend stories, and narrating. She had a talent for mimicry, and we've heard a number of accents from her over the years, with Beckett encouraging her. The two of them would play happily together for hours.

❦

Throughout these years, we still had our snow-removal business. It was not unusual for John to pack up the kids and take them plowing and salting with him while I was at work. They were happy for the adventures, sometimes slept through it all, but never seemed to mind heading out with their dad. John and I made the decision when the kids started school that we couldn't continue to interrupt nighttime routines.

❦

Since I worked rotating schedules, I would tell the children every day what they could expect. "Mommy won't be here when you wake up tomorrow, but I'll be back by dinner." Or, "Mommy will get you breakfast and lunch, and then Daddy will be home and he'll make you dinner and put you to bed." Even if we were running errands, I would tell them the order of errands before we ever left. Was I just doing it because they were young, to give them a sense of control? Or was I picking up cues from them and adjusting to their needs? I'll never know the answer to that question.

Learning & Games

We used baby signs with them, and they used them with us. I sometimes get asked if they had a twin language of their own. No, but surprisingly, April and I did. She would babble away, and I would answer her the same way, and our conversations would go on and on with her happy as a clam. I would swear that we understood each other perfectly.

When the children were little, we watched a lot of Baby Einstein. I used to sit with them, talking throughout the DVDs, pointing out and naming all the various animals, colors, whatever. I can't even begin to enumerate the number of educational DVDs I purchased and watched with them. I would play counting games, but April would not count with me. Not once.

One day after we had a large cookout, I was out in the backyard with the children when they started taking the leftover soda cans out of the cooler and placing them on the picnic table. The twins organized the cans in a row by color. Just as I was getting ready to tell them to put the cans away, I saw April point to each one, counting out loud all the way up to thirty-four.

Counting games would not be the last time we would see April refuse to practice new skills with someone. Instead she would wait until she felt confident in her knowledge before letting us see it. Sometimes the only way I could get her to answer a question as simple as "What animal is this?" was to counteract her silence with a crazy answer. "I know; it's an elephant." Then I *might* get the proper response: "Mommy, it's a gorilla. You're just being silly."

Beckett, on the other hand, has always loved to show off what he's learned. He was correctly typing out words and phrases on my computer by two years of age. On their second birthday, he typed the word *alphabet* correctly. Remember the computer programs from earlier? In self-defense, I started leaving Microsoft Word open on my computer for them to play with while I was at work. Each day I would change the font, size, and color; each evening I would find something new they had learned.

⌘

April would become extremely upset when she lost at games, especially board games. She would cry and scream. This would continue into her elementary school years.

Whenever it was available on a DVD or television show, we turned on the closed-captioning. My reasoning was that if they were going to be sitting in front of the TV, then they were going to see words too. Imagine my surprise the day April read the word *screaming* from the screen, a description of what was happening, not what was being said. Beckett would be inconsolable whenever closed-captioning wasn't available. "Letters, Mommy! I want letters!" Both kids were reading before kindergarten.

One time we were out on the pool deck and had the hose running for the kids to play with. Beckett picked it up, and from about ten feet away, John stepped on the hose to stop the waterflow. Beckett looked into the end, so, of course, John released the pressure so Beckett would get a faceful of water and laugh. This went on a number of times, with me saying to my husband, "You are such a dad; no mom would do that to her child." A little later, April picked up the hose and John repeated the process with her. She looked down the length of the hose to see John standing on it and gave him a sour look. It only took once for her to figure it all out. She has never put a hose end near her face since. Smart girl.

Outings

I freely admit that I was an overprotective parent in some ways. Whenever we went to theme parks, renaissance fairs, or museums, I always took a picture of the kids before we went in so that if something happened, I had a recent picture with what they were wearing. Back then, we called it my "in case Mommy and Daddy get lost" picture. Now, the kids will remind me to take the picture when we go certain places.

⚬

Restaurants could be hit or miss for us. At one particular restaurant, April would be under the table within five minutes every time. We correctly identified the source of her discomfort—too much echoing noise—but not the reason it affected her so deeply.

John and I would also have to curtail the length of our visits at holiday gatherings, family reunions, and large parties when April became overstimulated. There was one party at a location unfamiliar to the children with a large backyard. Beckett had gone deep in the yard to play and explore and when he decided to come back, I could see him becoming very distressed that he couldn't see me in the crowd. After that, I started to make sure that I wore a brightly colored shirt or jacket when we went to similar events.

⚬

We took the kids to a heavy-equipment show a couple times, where there was always an area set up for children: a large sandpit with toys for scooping and dumping dirt and a slight mound to climb. Beckett and April happily played in the dirt. At one point, John drew my attention to April, who had climbed the mound and was looking down at everyone else with her hands on her hips. He said, "She's decided to take on a supervisory role; she's standing just like you do sometimes."

⚬

Fortunately, our children were, and still are, exceptionally good travelers on car trips. While a minivan would have come in handy at times, higher gas prices and my long commute would have made it a poor financial decision when we could use a smaller vehicle with better gas mileage. What John and I did do, however, was rent minivans for weekend trips and vacations. We decided that if we ever got to the point where what we were paying in rentals in a year exceeded what six months of car payments would cost, we would purchase a minivan.

There was only one occasion when the children became cranky on a car trip. We had driven to New England in an ice storm for a funeral, and on that trip, I think we spent over thirty-two hours in the minivan over two days. I ended up having to sing continuously for over eight hours on the ride home to keep the kids calm. I had no voice the following day.

Since we had twins, shopping was a chore. I would always park near a cart return even if it meant I had to walk longer distances. That precaution meant I wouldn't have to leave them in their car seats unattended. To make the shopping more bearable, I would deliberately plan shopping trips with them when they weren't tired, had been fed, etc., to minimize everyone's potential for irritability. Actually, I think it's something most parents do when they can; no one likes shopping with a cranky child.

Overall, it worked fairly well for us. There was only one occasion when I had no choice but to do some Christmas shopping during nap-time, since it was my only semi-free time. I spent an hour, walking through the department store, chanting "Santa, Santa, Ho-Ho-Ho," a line from one of the movies they liked, desperately trying to keep them both entertained and calm. I'm sure I looked like a crazed lunatic to the other shoppers, but at least my kids weren't screaming and crying.

If you have children, you know the feeling as a parent that nothing is ever just yours again. With our children, they had a bad habit of taking a sip of whatever I was drinking as they passed by, then moving on again. With my job as an air traffic controller, I was subject to random breathalyzer and drug tests. Although federal law was less restrictive on the amount of time you could imbibe before a work shift, I made my personal standard twenty-four hours prior. It wasn't worth the risk of losing my career to have a few drinks.

On one of the rare occasions that we attended a family party when I did not have to work the next day, I decided I could have a few alcoholic drinks. John rarely imbibes, so I also had a designated driver. Unfortunately, Beckett came along and quickly took a sip from my cup before I could tell him not to. He spit it out and asked what it was. I told him. For months afterward, any time he went to take a sip from my cup, he would ask, "Is there alcohol in this?" He would come back five minutes later to the same cup and ask again. It didn't matter where we were, he would ask, and I would respond, "No." I finally had to tell him to stop because it sounded as if I had a drinking problem to others. I had to make a promise that I would tell him before I drank alcohol so he would know in advance not to touch my drink.

The twins were still in a double stroller the year John was scheduled for a colonoscopy. The facility required that John have someone waiting during the entire visit, and we had no one to watch the kids. So, we packed up the kids with the requisite diaper bags. The children and I had some quality time in the doctor's office while John had his procedure. When John was in recovery, they called me back. Six women—John's physician and five nurses—excitedly converged on the stroller squealing, "John told us the twins were here; let us see them!" Beckett, in the front seat, just smiled his beatific smile, happy with all the attention. April screamed at the top of her lungs, and there I was, saying quickly, "Everyone take two steps away from my daughter; and no, you can't hold her. You can pass him around though."

Comfort, Routines, & Family Traditions

As a toddler, Beckett loved to wrap himself tightly in an afghan or blanket, essentially swaddling himself. While he chose to do so quite often for no discernible reason, it did seem to calm him when he was upset. He still occasionally does it to this day.

I would make up silly songs for them. One of their favorites was a song I sang whenever they had been hurt falling down or bumping into things. I would be able to judge the level of pain from an injury by whether they were still crying by the time I finished the short ditty.

Bedtime routines included negotiations for how many books John and I would have to read as well as how many songs I would have to sing. If I was working night shifts, John was on his own. I've never asked, but I'm fairly certain he wasn't encouraged to sing.

❧

We inadvertently taught the children to anthropomorphize their stuffed toys by naming each one from the time they played on a floor mat. Some had their own distinct personalities, such as Horatio—a small monkey—who liked to play jokes. Kitty Cat and Puppy Dog were favorites and make an occasional appearance even now. Auntie Karen gave each of them a stuffed Mickey Mouse for their first birthday. It wasn't long before April commandeered both Mickeys, and they went everywhere with her up until she started pre-K. Orik (pronounced Orc) was a Pittsburgh Penguins Pillow Pet that April considered her best non-Beckett friend in elementary school. I used our stuffed toys in some of my social stories. The children began naming our cars and even our Christmas trees.

❧

Until I eventually retired, John and I often felt as if we were ships passing in the night (or day). Unless it was a weekend and I didn't have to work, most of our face-to-face interactions involved one of us coming home from work with the other sharing what needed to be done and the other packing up to head off to work. I looked forward to those few days and vacations when the entire family could be together.

Beyond regular phone calls during work breaks to connect, John and I began ensuring that on those few mornings we were both home and had nowhere to be, we would spend some time cuddling in bed, talking or laughing. When the children were younger, they joined us to interact for a while before heading off to play by themselves. Our habit continues to this day and occasionally one child will come in to grab a hug of his/her own. The tradition has helped us model a strong, loving marital relationship for our children.

❧

Toileting

No chapter on the early years with autism would be complete without some poop stories. Beckett pretty much potty-trained himself very early since he didn't like the feel of diapers. April had been mostly potty-trained, but then suffered a bad stomach virus, and a lot of that progress went by the wayside. April would use the potty reliably to urinate, but was resistant to using it to move her bowels. We used Pull-Ups for a time and at pre-K, but would put her in underwear during the day at home. She would use the potty to pee, but would poop in her underwear. The thing was, if we let her run around with no underwear or Pull-Up, she would use the potty for both, so we knew it wasn't a bodily control issue. We needed to get her to use the toilet *and* have underwear on during the day.

One day while I was at work, I got a call from John; he was furious with her. She had pooped twice in her underwear, and he got frustrated and yelled at her. He left her literally butt-naked so he wouldn't have to wash out yet another pair of undies. The next time she had to go, she went and put on a pair of undies, stood in front of him and moved her bowels. He could barely speak through his anger at her deliberate act of defiance and retribution for having been yelled at, and all I could do was laugh. I told him he was not going to win the battle; she held all the control in this arena. It was even funnier to me because John is usually the extremely patient parent, while I'm a little quicker to raise my voice.

Somewhere along the line, April started sleeping in her clothes instead of changing into pajamas, then putting on new clothes in the morning.

Oh, one more (cute) poop story, and then I'll stop, I promise. We were road tripping somewhere on vacation, and April was constipated when we stopped at a rest area in the middle of the night. I was in the stall with her, encouraging her to push it out. She suddenly smacked the top of her head like it was the bottom of a ketchup bottle and she could tap out what was stuck. I still get tears in my eyes laughing when I remember it. Our girl has always had a mechanical bent and an innate ability to figure out how things work.

❧

If you have any previous experience with autism, you may have recognized some of the early indicators of ASD in a number of the behaviors I described in this chapter. Hindsight can be a wonderful thing. However, we still didn't know we were living with autism and would not know for several years.

CHAPTER 4

EARLY INTERVENTION

This way and that; to and fro

Worlds expanding

And away they go...

A S I HAVE mentioned, either John or I were home caring for Beckett and April for the first four years of their lives. We lived on a busy street, but there weren't many children near their age on our side of the road. Unless they spent time with their cousins at a family gathering, they usually only played with each other or us. So, we decided to send them to full-day pre-K for a year before kindergarten to help them get used to being away from us.

We found one we really liked, not as close as some, but the teachers, staff, and the procedures they had in place appealed to us. By the children's accounts, they loved going there, and we got to hear about all their adventures. The only time I can recall one of them being upset was on picture day. The photographer had ABC blocks, with the *B* block being large enough for the children to sit upon. April was devastated because Beckett got to sit on the *B* block, while she wasn't allowed to sit on the smaller *A* block for her picture. In her mind, that was only right and fair. That's one of the few things she remembers about pre-K.

In the meantime, we began thinking about kindergarten. When we first purchased our home, we had deliberately chosen one in a good public-school district. However, a couple towns away, there was a pricey private school with an excellent reputation that I had started to think might be appropriate. Our children were smart, and I didn't want them to be bored in school like I had been. We took tours and were impressed with the poise and confidence of the students. We had no idea how we might pay for it without scholarships, but we put it on our list.

A couple months after they started pre-K, we were pulled aside by one of their teachers, Miss Lisa. She informed us that she was trained in early intervention and she had noted some behaviors that suggested April might benefit from testing. We were taken aback. What behaviors?

April was not interacting with the other children, although she might engage in parallel play. She rarely spoke unless it was to an adult, and even then, she was extremely soft spoken. She did not want to take part in a number of activities. The list wasn't very long, but John and I were confused. We hadn't seen any of this at home or at any family gatherings. There was only one behavior we saw both at home and at pre-K: her resistance to answering questions. She would often respond with "No" or "I don't know," even when we all knew she knew the answer.

We talked with John's sister, who had children close in age to ours, and asked if we could drop the kids off for a couple hours to get her take on April's behavior without us there. She was happy to agree. Afterwards, she said the teacher had been correct. April was quiet, resistant to playing with her cousins, but was fine interacting with her, although she used a low, hesitant voice.

So, we filled in the answers to the questionnaires and allowed the testing. The result was *social development delay*. We began an early intervention program with her at the pre-K. Beyond making more trips to the town park and encouraging her to interact with other children, there was no program suggested for home. April made some progress, but

CHAPTER 5

YOUR DAUGHTER
ISN'T AUTISTIC

Eyes open, eyes closed

Lights off, lights on

What you experience depends

On what side of the fence you're on…

LONG BEFORE OUR children attended public school, I had done my part lobbying in our state for a parent's right to choose whether or not their twins (or other multiples) were in the same or separate classrooms. I had read horror stories of districts around the country who arbitrarily did one or the other without any regard for what was truly best for the children. That bill passed and was signed into law before Beckett and April started school. It was briefly suggested by a guidance counselor that we separate the twins for kindergarten "so that they would begin to understand that they were individuals." Our response was simply, "They are not emotionally ready to be separated, and there is no doubt in anyone's mind, including theirs, that they are individuals."

Because April was transitioning from Early Intervention to the public school system, additional testing was required. We met with representatives from the school district to determine how best to accomplish it. Would she feel more comfortable with a man or woman? Was age a factor? What would motivate her to cooperate? And so on. We made all the decisions, answered all the questionnaires and waited to hear back.

The day for the results came, and the district representative, a young man, spoke with John and me about their findings. He pretty much told us that, yes, April qualified for services. He informed us her diagnosis was *pervasive developmental disorder, not otherwise specified* (PDD-NOS), and she would receive support from the autistic classroom. He stressed repeatedly that April did not have autism, and to please not become upset, but it was the only classification that would ensure she would receive the aid she required. He seemed concerned that we were going to become unreasonable over the word *autism*. I finally said, "So, what you're saying is that it's the same thing as social development delay but with a different name?" He said yes.

During our discussion, he made it sound as if we just had to get her up to speed with her peers socially and then she wouldn't require services or additional support anymore. I'm still not certain if I should be angry with him for giving us false information, whether knowingly or not, or thank him.

CHAPTER 6

THE FIRST COUPLE YEARS NOT BEING AUTISTIC

Take care of my little ones

Away from me

Love first, teach second

Hearts and minds open to see.

AFTER THE SCHOOL district agreed that April qualified for support services, we wrote her first IEP. In truth, for
that first plan, John and I pretty much went with the district's recommendations.

As an involved mom, I have emailed our children's teachers at the
beginning of each school year with information about the kids—likes,
dislikes, strengths, weaknesses, etc.—to ensure their educators knew that
I considered them part of our team and that the lines of communication
were always open. I have found that not all educators respond to that
initial contact, but most do appreciate it, whether they take the time to
answer or not. One line that has been in there for every educator: "April
is a very intelligent, imaginative, and funny child ... who is probably

going to make you absolutely crazy at times, even as she makes you laugh. She is very much a kinesthetic/auditory learner."

When April was initially diagnosed as PDD-NOS, there wasn't much information available on the internet about it; there still isn't. I would search and re-search, but I found myself frustrated and not much better informed than when we had started. If ASD were on a scale, rather than a spectrum, April would be placed a tad above Asperger's. She was able to spend most of her school day in the general education classrooms, but required frequent breaks.

⁓

Their kindergarten teacher remains one of my favorites to this day. I used to say that it was because she was the only other person besides me to survive both my twins all day, every day. Looking back, now knowing what I know about how April's autism manifested in school then, I am profoundly grateful to her for all the love and support she showered on our kids, all the while doing the same for all the other children in the class.

⁓

Sunny, April's support teacher at the time, was absolutely fabulous. She would communicate with me regularly, letting me know what changes she thought were needed to help our daughter. One of those changes to her IEP included adding a mandatory break in the early afternoon, since, as Sunny said, "It's just too difficult for April to hold it together for a full day."

"How can we solve the problem?" became our mantra at home and at school. All of the adults would ask April this question after meltdowns. Most times we had to guide her to an answer or suggest a solution and attempt to get her input.

Manifestations

By now, April would throw herself to the floor crying during a meltdown, regardless of location. Her crippling anxiety became a much bigger worry for us. Each school year was preceded by weeks of her crying daily, certain that her teachers would hate her.

Choices became painful, even what color crayon to use; she worried that she'd make the wrong choice even when gently reminded there was no such thing. When she was unsure of the proper response, either socially or for her schoolwork, she would get a deer-in-the-headlights look on her face and begin hiding or turtling into her shirt. When she became overly stressed or overwhelmed, she'd cry and be unable to speak. Her throat literally would close up, and she would be unable to make any sounds; it still happens occasionally.

Unannounced changes in classroom routines upset her, including schedule changes required by half days or event days. This was the same child to whom John or I could say, "Hey, let's pack up and go on a surprise trip," and she would happily grab some favorite items, her shoes, and coat and we'd be out the door without further explanation and no distress.

April's stress would manifest in other ways as well. She would chew on her fingernails (or any other inanimate object in the vicinity). Both she and her brother would chew on everything; I used to joke that I was trying to raise children, not puppies. April would also pull threads from the tops of her socks and essentially floss her teeth with the threads.

April once had an incident on the school bus and didn't stay in her seat. When we questioned her about the bus rules, she knew them, but kept repeating she was afraid she would forget them. I made a keyring, similar to a flipchart, and put pictures and text showing one of the bus rules on each item on the keyring. I attached it to her backpack so she could have it available for reference. April has an excellent memory, and this was our first indicator that she had an incredible fear of not remembering the rules for school. She never used the keychain, but needed the security of having it there to reduce her anxiety, just in case.

᪐

Google Maps was an obsession for Beckett for quite some time, and he knew our area very well, expanding outwards for a couple towns. There were times we were out driving, and we would let him direct us so he could see various streets and neighborhoods in person. A few times at an unfamiliar intersection, I would ask him if I needed to turn right or left to get where we wanted to go because I wasn't sure. We still call him our human GPS.

Family

Our morning bus routine ritual included a final hug and kiss. "Have a great day" was always added by John or me. The kids would sometimes reply, "Have a fun day at work." I was still "Mommy" to both children.

While we might have occasionally swatted one of them on a diapered bottom to reinforce a safety-related rule, when they tried to run off in parking lot or something similar, spanking as a punishment was not something John and I had considered a good practice. There was one occasion April had done something fairly serious—I honestly can't remember what it was; I only remember the events afterward. I gave her the choice of going to bed without dinner or a spanking, fully expecting she would pick the former. I was wrong.

Now I was in the position of having to follow through, which I did not like at all, but it was my fault for suggesting it in the first place. After two swats, April said, "I think I've changed my mind." I responded, "It doesn't work that way; you can't change your mind," and gave her a couple more swats. I regretted it and hated that I was stupid enough to put myself in that position; I never offered it as an option again. Unfortunately, I think it's going to be one of those memories that sticks around for all of us.

Sports

John and I enrolled both kids in soccer, as well as T-ball for Beckett and softball for April. Soccer only lasted two seasons. Softball was one season for April; she just would not participate reliably. Beckett's T-ball team had an opening his second year, and the coach allowed April to take the spot. Once we realized that it was likely that our children were going to get physically hurt from not paying attention during practices and games, we finished the season and looked for other options. We had a pool and spent as much time in it as weather and schedules allowed. Both children loved the water, but neither expressed any interest in joining a local swim team.

The children participated in mixed martial arts (MMA) for years, and while both did well overall, it never did become something they were passionately interested in. They learned self-defense skills, and we had meaningful discussions about our expectations on when and where it was appropriate to use which skills. Their last year in MMA, during junior high, it became a battle to get them to go to practices, so we decided to drop that sport too.

I added PTA (parent-teacher association) volunteering to my ever-increasing list of activities and responsibilities. I ended up on the local unit boards for most of our children's school years up through the start of high school. Beyond the fact that I cared about all the students, it had the added benefit of allowing me to develop lasting relationships with the teachers and staff. I might see a teacher in the school halls or during an event, and they would bring up something about one of my children, asking for advice or extra support at home for an assignment. I learned things about my children that I may not have otherwise. I may have been tired most days, but I think it was worth it.

CHAPTER 7
THE REALIZATION

On you, my eyes, my nose,
My feet, my toes,
But all yours, not mine
The world to divine.

BECAUSE THEY WERE emotionally ready, John and I separated Beckett and April in first grade. The separation would give April more opportunities to interact with classmates other than her brother. One day when they were in second grade, I was working at the PTA's Santa's Workshop. In the afternoon, April and her general education teacher came up to me. Our daughter's teacher told me that April's support teacher was handling another situation and asked if it would it be okay if April sat with me awhile for a break. Well, of course, my daughter is always welcome to be with me.

April had quiet tears running down her face and she was holding her entire little body in tightly, all the while vibrating with tension. I asked her teacher if my daughter was like this every day and found out, to my shock and dismay, that this was what "not able to hold it together" looked and felt like for her. Never before had I seen April like that, and the knowledge that I had had absolutely no idea of the extent to which she suffered every school day was sobering. I felt like the worst parent ever.

This time, it was her support teacher who talked me off my guilt-ridden-parent ledge. Sunny hadn't known that John and I were parenting under a different set of assumptions, based on erroneous information given to us after April's district assessment. Sunny reassured me that we had been doing the correct things to support our daughter in coping with her challenges. In essence she told me that while we may not have understood all along that April truly did have autism and what that meant for her long-term, we knew our daughter well and had made all the right decisions to this point.

While I did feel better to a certain extent, it wasn't until years later that I really forgave myself for my ignorance. I was talking with another parent who was dealing with her own mom guilt as it pertained to one of her neurotypical children and told her, "You can't continue to beat yourself up about it. All we can do as parents is do the best we can with the information we have and change course as our knowledge deepens." I sincerely meant my words and realized as I said them that I needed to take them to heart myself.

Unfortunately, when I tell people that April lives with high-functioning autism, many mistakenly assume autism itself affects her to a lesser degree than other autistic people. What it really means is that her autism affects the neurotypical world around her less. What she copes with is much more internal and quite often invisible to others. Now that she is a little older, and in many ways presents as neurotypical, people can be surprised when she does have difficulties coping.

I would bet most, if not all, parents of autistic children have heard someone say, "You should discipline your child more," when a meltdown has occurred in public. We parents are put in a position of having to choose whether to educate the less-than-compassionate bystander or find ways to help our child. Unless we have someone else with us who can take on some of the load, our child will be the priority. What has always irritated me about such comments is that many neurotypical children also have meltdowns in public for some of the same reasons as autistic children and the comments are just as unfair to those families as it is to ours.

CHAPTER 8

RESEARCH & SCARY STATISTICS

How could I not know?

The beat of my heart

Forgive me, my love,

As we go back to the start...

AFTER MY REALIZATION that our daughter truly was autistic, I had different parameters for my research, so research I did; I still do. I began gaining a much deeper understanding of what April experiences on a daily basis and the challenges and obstacles she faces, not only in the short-term, but also in the long-term. I learned that PDD-NOS was more commonly referred to *atypical autism* in the old classification system before all autism disorders were combined under ASD in 2013, which is why I had had difficulty finding information on it. I learned the all-too-accurate phrase, "If you've met one person with autism, you've met one person with autism."

My understanding is that there are seven primary areas where difficulties occur to some degree for an autistic individual. The most important things to remember are that someone with autism experiences some difficulties in each of these areas (some areas much more than others) and that many of these areas of function overlap with one another. For example, significant difficulties with sensory processing, especially with a number of senses involved, can also create increased difficulties with social awareness, repetitive behaviors, neuro-motor skills, information processing, etc.

⋘

Individuals with autism experience difficulties in the following seven areas:

1. Information processing
   a. Ability to assimilate and utilize/apply new information quickly
      i. Sees/experiences details before the "big picture"
      ii. Difficulties remembering sequences of tasks
      iii. Difficulties understanding that other people may think, feel, or have perspectives different to their own
   b. Adapting to new environments/situations
   c. Includes literal language; may not understand humor, irony, or metaphoric phrases or have difficulties with abstract concepts
   d. Difficulties communicating needs and desires
2. Monotropic mindset
   a. Narrow, but intense, ability to focus creating difficulties changing/switching tasks and sometimes resulting in perseveration (obsessive interests)
   b. *Theory of mind* difficulties, as the narrow focus decreases the focus on the attentional demands of social cues
3. Neuro-motor differences
   a. Ability to control bodily movements
   b. Can range from jerkiness or clumsiness to an inability to intentionally move the body
   c. Sensory input affects neuro-motor function

4. Pragmatic language
   a. Social communication, including body language, eye contact, small talk, and turn-taking in conversation
   b. Using appropriate strategies for gaining attention and interrupting, asking for or offering assistance, intonation of voice, body distance/personal space
5. Repetitive behaviors
   a. Stims can be beneficial or harmful
   b. Can be verbal or physical
6. Sensory processing
   a. Seven senses
      i. Hearing
      ii. Proprioception (relative position of parts of the body and strength of effort being employed in movement)
      iii. Sight
      iv. Smell
      v. Sound
      vi. Taste
      vii. Vestibular (perception of body in relation to gravity, movement, and balance)
   b. Can be hyposensitive (too little) or hypersensitive (too much) to sensory stimuli
7. Social Awareness, Behavior and Understanding
   a. Ability to form and maintain relationships
      i. Unlikely to pursue social interaction
      ii. Difficulty approaching others; detached and aloof
      iii. Difficulty making friends with peers
      iv. Resistant to being touched
   b. Ability to (intuitively) pick up/understand social cues, norms, taboos, etiquette, etc.
      i. Unusual or inappropriate facial expressions, body language, and expressions

≼

There is a broad range of mental skills called *executive function* that helps people interact with others and complete tasks. While many people assume these skills are simply organizational skills, they are not. Planning is important, yes, but recognizing the need for plans, actually initiating them, flexibility in changing them as required, and completing them in a timely fashion are all part of this life-skill set.

Here is a short list of some of the mental skills encompassed by executive function:

1. Analyzing information
2. Concentrating
3. Controlling behavior
4. Controlling emotions
5. Controlling mental focus
6. Multitasking
7. Organization
8. Planning
9. Problem solving
10. Processing information
11. Remembering details
12. Time management

The prefrontal cortex of the brain plays a large role in executive function skills, impulse control, and personality development. Executive function skills need to be taught to every child, neurotypical or autistic, but in many instances, learning such skills creates significant difficulties for those with autism.

For example, April demonstrates fairly good short-term executive function skills in her schoolwork. If she has homework assigned early in her school day and finds herself with free time during a subsequent class, she will initiate, and many times complete, the homework long before she ever arrives home. However, at home, she requires reminders from us to begin homework or start on chores, and rarely will she independently initiate needed tasks that she does not have an interest in, such as picking up items from the floor or feeding the cat. She and Beckett both require assistance reverse-engineering a timeline for larger school projects or goals, and neither can reliably be trusted to start those projects or goals and keep on track on their own without prompts. I would estimate that only 5% of the time will April remember to comb her hair after a shower without a reminder. It was only after she got braces that she was able to remember to brush her teeth without a reminder. Hopefully, that will continue even after her braces are removed.

Despite her high intelligence, without sufficient executive function skills being developed, our daughter may not be able to live independently in the future. Beyond basic grooming, there are things like being able to manage a personal schedule of getting up and ready on time, ensuring the grocery shopping is done, dishes and laundry washed and put away, paying bills on time, and forgoing fun activities earlier to ensure an appropriate bedtime to get a decent night's rest before it starts all over again. And those are just a few of the many activities that require adequate executive function skills.

We're still working to find the right combinations of methods that work to foster our children's growth in this area—charts, planners, signs, reward systems, etc.—but as of yet, it is still an uphill battle. Every child is different; our children are certainly smart enough and physically capable, but there are weaknesses in these critical skills. Right now, we're attempting a combination of a motivated self-interest and delayed gratification strategy: no more reminders for homework, but if homework is not completed by dinnertime, then no electronics after dinner for the remainder of the evening. When they become reliably proficient with that, we will slowly add additional necessary tasks to the list.

⋨

According to Harvard University's Center on the Developing Child, *toxic stress response* can occur when a child experiences strong, frequent, and/or prolonged adversity and seriously delay or impair his/her executive function skills development. As you read the following paragraphs, you may question whether autistic difficulties with executive function originate in the brain at birth, are exacerbated by an individual's fight-or-flight response, or are actually created by an individual's fight-or-flight response in the earliest years of life. I do not know the answer to the question, but I do know that the fight-or-flight response has made it much harder to teach executive function skills to our children.

⤸

The *fight-or-flight response* (or *acute stress syndrome*) is a survival response all of us have experienced at one point or another. It begins in the amygdala, part of the brain's limbic system. The limbic system is where a lot of our emotional processing, as well as recognizing facial expressions, takes place, and it is often referred to as the feeling and reacting portion of the brain. When the amygdala perceives a threat via sensory means, it sends messages to the hypothalamus and hippocampus, other parts of the limbic system.

The hypothalamus controls our autonomic nervous system, which is why we might get sweaty palms, feel our hearts race, feel our muscles tense up, or a whole host of other physical symptoms, many times before we've even consciously registered the perceived threat. The hippocampus, meanwhile, turns short-term memories into long-term memories and reminds us which emotional reactions are congruent with our mood. For many neurotypical adults, the prefrontal cortex, the decision-making portion of our brain, follows up shortly thereafter to decide the appropriate steps to take, if any, or makes the decision to calm our bodies. All this can take place in a matter of seconds or even milliseconds.

In a single second, the subconscious mind can absorb 20 million bits of information through its senses. In a neurotypical mind, that data is filtered down to only seven to forty bits for the conscious mind. I have not yet found any research that states how much an autistic mind filters the subconscious data for the conscious mind, but I would be willing to bet it is higher than 40 bits or more consistently at the high end of that range for most autistic people, contributing to sensory overload.

Perceived threats do not have to be a true life-or death-threat (e.g., a speeding car headed your way, a piano falling on you), but threats that an individual simply might be fearful of to some degree (public speaking, heights, spiders, test-taking, etc.). This is very important to know when aiding people with autism; when their brains trigger the fight-or-flight response, they are reacting to what their senses tell them is a threat to their own survival. I remember hearing about an autistic child in elementary school some years ago who was huddled in a corner, eyes tightly shut, hands over ears, screaming, "Make it stop! Please make it stop!" This child was not trying to be disruptive or deliberately misbehaving; instead his/her survival instincts were in overdrive from his/her body's fight-or-flight response triggered by sensory overload.

Those with high emotional regulation and low emotional reactivity to an event reach the prefrontal cortex stage more quickly and are able to make more appropriate decisions based upon the level of threat perceived. My ability to deal with rapidly changing or emergency situations, especially as an air traffic controller, has served me and the flying public well. However, I have discovered over the years that it is as if my amygdala sends messages directly to my prefrontal cortex first, before sending it to any other areas of my limbic system. I would deal with emergency situations just fine, but when all was said and done, I would then suffer the physical effects of my autonomic nervous system kicking in. I know of no body of research that would support this theory or if somewhere along the line, I instinctively learned to suppress my autonomic nervous system and emotional responses long enough to deal with perceived threats. Either way, in most instances, my emotions take a back seat to what needs to be done at the time.

There is a whole host of research that shows that a teenager's brain does not process information with the prefrontal cortex (rational part) but rather the amygdala (emotional part). In fact, until age twenty-five, a teenager's brain won't be fully developed in the prefrontal cortex area, which helps to explain some of the poor decisions we made when we were younger. But it also explains why children and young adults with autism have difficulties with emotional regulation, impulse control, and executive function.

∽

The amygdala plays an important role in autism, but as of yet, no one can definitively say why. My hypothesis is that it is not that the amygdala is damaged in any way, but instead hyperactive or hypoactive, and possibly experiences connectivity issues with other parts of the brain. We already know sensory processing is an issue for those with autism. In the cases of hypersensitivity, there is simply too much input to filter effectively in a short period of time, while hyposensitivity may not give enough information to someone to process correctly.

In April's case, it seems like there is an eight-lane superhighway between her amygdala and hippocampus, while in neurotypicals, it may only be a two-lane road. It appears to me that her superhighway is so wide and traffic is moving so fast, she cannot always find the exit ramp for her prefrontal cortex in time.

Regardless, limbic system responses are exceedingly strong for those with autism, and dare I say, overwhelmingly tenacious in retaining control instead of letting the prefrontal cortex participate quickly in any given stressful situation. This is why *emotional regulation* is a term you will hear a lot as a parent of an autistic child. Because the amygdala (emotional part) of the brain is perceiving threats—be it loud noises, an incessant hum, having to attempt to socialize, etc.—it triggers an instinctive and primal emotional response to keep the individual safe. For some, that emotional response is primarily anxiety; for others, primarily anger. If a person cannot manage the emotion(s) effectively, the prefrontal cortex does not get a chance to do its job and think it through.

The best thing you can do for someone with autism at this point is simply to help them calm their emotions and bodies. Questions, explanations, and logic will have no positive effect on them until their emotional response has been managed, and may have the opposite of the intended effect by increasing their stress-level response.

April's emotional fight-or-flight response is anxiety, while Beckett's is anger, mostly at himself. For a long time, while coming back from a meltdown, April would say things like I don't deserve to live, I don't deserve to exist, I don't deserve to live in a house, I'm a bad person, or I don't deserve to be loved—all part of the hippocampus' emotional response. Black and white, good and bad, yin and yang. The struggle to learn or accept components of gray in all abstract things is very, very real, especially for most autistic people and is exacerbated during a fight-or-flight episode.

Beckett still stomps away like an elephant when he is feeling criticized or that he has disappointed an authority figure or himself. While we are pleased that he is able to recognize that he isn't ready or capable of handling the intense emotions at the time and removes himself from a situation, we still have a long way to go to get him to the point of being able to discuss it calmly afterwards. Emotional regulation for both children is something we continue to work to improve.

⚶

Everyone experiences stress at different points in their lives, and short periods or small amounts of stress are not harmful to us. Cognitive, emotional, and physical symptoms of stress include racing thoughts, constant worrying, disorganization, feeling overwhelmed, difficulty quieting your mind, low self-esteem, headaches, chest pain, and insomnia. And that is just the short list of possible symptoms.

However, long-term stress can decrease life span and negatively impact quality of life. It is well-documented that chronic, ongoing stress adversely affects a person's mental, cardiovascular, and gastrointestinal health as well contributing to other issues.

We already know that sensory overload creates fight-or-flight stress responses for those with ASD, starting at birth. Essentially, increasing the ability to regulate emotions, self-advocate, and garnering executive function skills all lead back to managing stress.

In my opinion, our primary focus should be aiding autistic people in learning to manage their stress and finding ways that work for them to keep their stress at consistently lower levels. It affects every aspect of their short-term and long-term health.

When making choices for our children on our journey with autism, I keep this guidepost first and foremost in my view. It is far more important to me that our children live long, happy, healthy lives than whether or not they appear normal to the neurotypical world.

I learned about applied behavioral analysis therapy (ABA), which can improve social, communication, and learning skills through (mostly) positive reinforcement. However, the more I learned, the less I felt it was a good fit for our daughter as it seemed to focus primarily on normalizing behaviors (or symptoms, if you will) of autism and not on understanding and addressing the root causes of those behaviors. I know some families who have utilized ABA and felt it met their child's needs, and I am happy for them.

While John and I have utilized some of the concepts of ABA therapy, like a reward system for certain behaviors, such as completing chores, those have been utilized in the same way any parent might use them rather than with the goal of eradicating any outsider's view of our child's autism. And how could we, in good conscience, force—or encourage with rewards—our child to have unwanted physical contact (in the forms of hugs or kisses) in the hopes of appearing "normal" to the neurotypical world when we also were teaching our children that their bodies are their own and no one was allowed to touch them in ways that make them feel uncomfortable?

One teacher suggested we think about medicating April to help with her anxiety. John and I had talked about it, but did not believe we were at the stage where we felt the potential risks were outweighed by any possible rewards. Being female and high-functioning, April might want to someday have children of her own. We were concerned we might be setting her up for an increased risk to her unborn children before she herself could make an informed choice in the matter. Additionally, some of the things we adore about our daughter are her quick, agile mind and her creativity and ability to see new things in everyday items; we worried that those traits would be dulled or even disappear with medication. Although, I admit I have bookmarked the appropriate pages for reference in Temple Grandin's book, *Thinking in Pictures, Expanded Edition: My Life with Autism*, in case we do ever decide that route is appropriate and necessary.

I have also learned that there is not nearly enough research or material dealing with the differences of gender in autism and how to address those differences in the home environment. On average, autistic girls seem to be better at *masking* or camouflaging their autism. Many girls develop a survival adaptation to hide what is going on inside them, which is probably one reason why boys are diagnosed with ASD at a greater frequency than girls. Girls require different things during puberty than boys do and require it a lot earlier.

A report from late 2018 printed in the *Journal of the American Academy of Child & Adolescent Psychiatry* states that there is a higher co-occurrence of gender diversity (identifying outside of the gender binary and sexuality) and autism. The reviewers looked at nineteen studies, of which only seven could be supported with clinical diagnoses of ASD (rather than reported ASD traits alone). When they reviewed those seven studies, they found that a clinical diagnosis of ASD is 4.1 to 17.5 times more likely to occur in those who identify as gender diverse than in the general population. In essence, identifying outside of conventional genders and sexualities is not unusual amongst those with autism.

During my initial research stage, I read somewhere that suicide rates before age thirty-eight for autistic people were incredibly high, with females being at higher risk. Today's research shows that in the United Kingdom, an autistic child is twenty-eight times more likely than neurotypical children to think about or attempt suicide, while autistic adults without a learning disability are nine times more likely than their neurotypical counterparts to die from suicide.[1] The results from a twenty-year Utah study released in early 2019 showed that autistic females had three times the risk of suicide than their neurotypical female counterparts.[2]

For the past two hours, I've been sitting here and attempting to determine how best to write this paragraph… or maybe I have been just avoiding it altogether because it is a soul-wrenching memory for me. During an IEP meeting when April was in third grade, her general education teacher told me that our daughter had said to her, "I'm not going to live to age sixteen." Silent tears ran down my face at the thought that one of the biggest parts of my heart walking around outside my body had even considered the idea that she might not live to adulthood… or might not want to.

John and I were eventually able to determine that April only has these thoughts during the worst of her meltdowns, but we have kept a close eye on her emotional state outside of fight-or-flight situations. We also began having many discussions about her telling us if she feels this way more than usual or ever feels compelled to act on those feelings. We continue to talk about seeing a psychiatrist and using medication if any of us, especially her, thinks it is time. In the meantime, we are quickly approaching age sixteen, and I hope we can continue to improve April's ability to regulate her emotions so that the most pernicious of self-destructive thoughts do not ever find fertile soil in which to take root and grow in her mind.

For those readers with ASD children with more needs than our family has had to address, I suggest that you continue your research into other therapies and services that I haven't mentioned, such as what forms of

1 www.autisca.org
2 Autism Research published by International Society for Autism Research published by Wiley Periodicals, Inc.

CHAPTER 9

MORE ON THE ELEMENTARY SCHOOL YEARS

At times so serious, others so fey,
My awe has no bounds
Witnessing your strength each day
In a world that confounds.

ONE OF THE things I like about our school district is that a great deal of caring thought goes into which classrooms are best suited for an individual child, as well as what other children may be in the same classroom. In April's case, her primary general education teachers for almost every year of elementary school had a special education certification and prior special education teaching experience. April was also placed in classes with children who were most likely to be kind and accepting.

In Beckett's case, one year there were four girls who ended up disliking each other intensely, and our son was caught in the verbal crossfire, with three of them practicing their future mean-girl skills by going out their way to make our sensitive Beckett cry and the other staunchly defending him. The next year saw Beckett and his protective friend in the same classroom and the others split amongst other classrooms. In all of these placements, the teachers, counselors, and administrative staff worked together to find the best fits without input from me, although I have no doubt that if I had stated a preference, it would have been seriously considered.

✦

The elementary school years were also the years when I developed chronic back pain, which was exacerbated by my long commute, crazy schedule, and the fact that I could not take anything stronger than ibuprofen within twenty-four hours of a work shift. Every three weeks I had a one-day weekend, which meant I could not receive any significant relief from the pain for ten days in a row. If I was experiencing a flare-up, especially during those long periods, I became irritable and impatient. I was aware of the problem, which helped to a degree, since I would let my children know early in the day that I knew I would be less patient than normal. But I could not help but feel guilty when I got frustrated or exasperated with my children faster than I would have liked.

Health

Although our children were mostly healthy, Beckett started getting multiple ear infections in kindergarten and needed surgery to implant tubes in his ears. Several months later, he fell off our bed while playing "robot" and broke his arm, which also required surgery to set. During a routine bloodwork test, we discovered that April would become very faint after giving blood, and we began ensuring we had snacks and drinks that she liked ready for her after any subsequent tests.

✦

April's autism adversely affects her physical coordination. As a toddler she fell and had a tooth pierce through her skin on two separate occasions. Her dance moves usually appear stiff and jerky. When she runs, her head and torso lean very far forward, and she streams her arms straight out behind her almost parallel to the ground, similar to Naruto running. She has difficulties with her vestibular sense and balance, has been unable to ride a bicycle, and refuses to attempt it again. However, with encouragement, April did participate in our county's Special Olympics each year she was asked in elementary school.

⌇

In third grade, a friend pulled me aside to tell me she thought Beckett might be experiencing absence seizures. They were fleeting and appeared to be triggered mostly when he was emotionally distressed. He went through a series of tests, all of which came back normal, which only told us he didn't have a seizure during the various tests and if he was having them, they had not left any permanent damage in his brain. The events typically lasted only three to five seconds, during which he just stopped all movement and speech except breathing. He would not be aware of the event, and sometimes would need prompting to remember what had been occurring beforehand. We haven't seen any since then and have discontinued testing for now. We believe that he might have been experiencing a time of abnormal brain growth, as they started immediately following a few months of night terrors, and once his internals equalized, the suspected seizures simply ceased. If you were not looking directly in his eyes at the time, you might never know he had one.

This was a scary time for our family, especially for April, knowing her brother was having these tests, which had him up very early, kept him from sleeping, and required an overnight stay in the hospital. We explained to the children that brain cells each have a job to do, and they talk to each about how and when to do those jobs via a form of electricity. We told them Beckett was being tested because we thought some of Beckett's brains cells might be getting rambunctious, loud and rowdy, and some of the other brain cells were becoming distracted by the first ones and forgetting what they were supposed to be doing, like helping Beckett walk, talk, etc. The explanation seemed to satisfy them and alleviate their worries.

Comfort, Routines, & Family

Sunny was able to obtain funds to set up a sensory area in the autistic classroom. This area quickly became a favorite place for April when she needed to calm herself at school. John and I hung mosquito netting over April's bed at home to recreate that calm, comfortable, safe space for her to go to whenever she felt she needed it.

April's comfort level with hugs varied. Her physical affection with us approximated what would be considered normal by the neurotypical world. But with others she cared about, it was a shorter duration, sideways-type affair with her turning her head and body mostly away, but trying. As she's aged, how she hugs a person, including us, depends on the situation and how stressed she is feeling.

Most parents look for and try to take advantage of teachable moments. If there were a Mom of the Day award, I would have felt I truly earned it the day I was able to link internet safety to Disney's *Frozen* after our kids had seen it. I had been trying to explain why it was important for our children to never give out their personal information or pictures online without our prior approval. Hans was a perfect character for them to relate to as someone misrepresenting himself and his motives for personal gain. Now that our children are teenagers, have cell phones, and are spending more time online in chatrooms and the like, they still remember this lesson from early on.

Third grade is also when April decided she might want to design video games and Beckett expressed wanting to be a professional animator/cartoonist. April's interest in designing video games has since waned, but Beckett's ambitions remain the same. It was also the year that my mother relocated from New England and she and my youngest brother lived with us for months. We had some deaths in our neighborhood very close together too.

Somewhere during this time frame, Beckett became fearful of sleeping alone and would crawl into bed with John and me every night (our master bedroom was on the ground floor with the twins' bedrooms upstairs). We would return him to his bed, stay with him until he fell back asleep, only to find him with us again later that night. We made beds for him on our floor to no avail. After weeks of interrupted sleep, John and I gave up and let him co-sleep with us since he obviously needed it, and our research showed that it would not harm him. After several months of Beckett co-sleeping, April decided that she didn't want to be alone either. It was very crowded in our queen (soon upgraded to a king) bed for a number of years. As the children grew, my aching back liked the situation less and less.

April became irritated with the lack of space first and moved to the living room couch for her bed. Eventually, we were able to get Beckett to sleep in his own bed by John and I moving into the guest bedroom upstairs so our son felt we were close. We left it up to Beckett as to when he felt comfortable enough for us to move back to our own bedroom, which took about a month. But now we had a problem getting April back to her room. Then I realized that it had changed to a sensory issue for her; she liked to sleep pressed up against the back of the couch. We moved her bed against the walls in a corner, purchased a long body pillow for her to put between her back and the wall, and finally, we had everyone sleeping where they should again.

Nighttime routines changed to the children and I taking turns reading from a book, usually one that was an encyclopedia of facts for whatever interests they shared, such as Ninjago or Pokemon characters. Cuddles were still necessary.

Beckett's art was becoming more complex, and April's creativity was con-tinually making itself known. During one of my nighttime calls home to say goodnight from work, John instructed me not to walk through the living room when I arrived home if I didn't want to be decapitated. Of course, when I got home, I had to turn the lights on to see what he had been talking about. April had created a zipline for her stuffed animals to play on from the curtain rods to a piece of furniture across the room. Another time, she, with Beckett's help, fashioned a pirate ship out of our living room couch – complete with portholes, cannons, and flags.

I had read an article that suggested it was impossible to maintain strong emotions when drawing. Since we were already concerned about April's handwriting, we encouraged her to draw as a means to improve her fine motor skills, to calm herself, and as an additional outlet to express her feelings. Unlike her brother, she was quite happy to use a sketchbook, although she would only rarely allow us to see what she had drawn.

I also rediscovered a love of crochet and began making all sorts of items. I had seen a pattern for a baby blanket that involved tripling the amount of bulky yarns. I decided to make larger versions for Beckett and April substituting with various fluffy soft yarns. The results were heavy, soft, and breathable, and I had unknowingly created our own weighted blankets before I had even heard the term. April still sleeps with one.

April started calling me Mom during these years. I was not emotionally ready for the change in nomenclature.

Manifestations

April liked to narrate or say the same things repeatedly. We began teaching her that three times was the most she could repeat herself because it was natural for other people to become uninterested at that point. After a second or third time of hearing the exact same monologue, we would ask her, "Was that two or three times? I can't remember." This helped to enhance her awareness of what she was saying and how often she was repeating herself. She still occasionally repeats herself, but she is able to self-regulate this particular behavior quite well now.

A common difficulty for autistic people, especially children, is recognizing when he/she needs help and asking for that aid or a break. Sunny made a Break card that April could place on her desk to communicate nonverbally to her general education teacher that she needed to visit Sunny. Many times, the two caring paraprofessionals who worked closest with our daughter or her general education teacher had to prompt April to use the card.

✑

Below, I've shared a number of emails exchanged with April's teachers during her first-grade year.

From: Me
To: Sunny and Mrs. Jackson (April's 1ˢᵗ grade teacher)
Date: November 20, 2011

Mrs. Jackson and Sunny,
Just wanted to let you know that I've been in the hospital since Friday afternoon. Nothing life-threatening - just that persistent cough that hasn't responded to home treatment.
April seems to be handling it well, considering, but she's been more vocal/sad about my not being home than Beckett. So, I wanted you both to have the heads-up just in case. I do have access to my email and cell phone while I'm here if we need to communicate. I'm not sure when I'll be released, but hoping before Thanksgiving.
Thanks,
Vivian

From: Sunny
To: Me
Date: February 10, 2012

I wanted to make you aware of some things that Mrs. Jackson and I have observed with April since we have returned from Christmas break. She has been coming to my room more frequently to regroup.

Mrs. Jackson has observed that she has been talking to herself and seems more withdrawn from her peers. Today April hid under her desk during recess and then cried when playtime was over because she didn't have the opportunity to play. When she came to my room, I asked her what made her hide and she said that another student said "boo" to her and that she then didn't know what to do. She has been particularly emotional this week. I am observing some social skill needs that I can address on my end in school. I may need to see her on a more consistent basis so that I can address her social skill needs. I will continue to keep you informed. As always, please feel free to share your insight with us.

Have a good weekend. :-)

Sunny

From: Me
To: Sunny
Date: February 10, 2012

I know April's been fighting off something since a week ago last Thursday. She'll be fine, then her temp will go up to 102. Whenever she's ill, she seems to regress. :-(I've noticed the increase in crying/distress this week as well. Her temp went up again tonight; looks like a doctor's appointment will be in order.

Since Christmas break, every few days she tries to find a reason that she has to stay home from school. She'll fake a cough, pretend her stomach hurts, etc. Usually, once I reiterate that staying home from school means no playing, no computer, etc., she decides she'd rather go to school. I've asked her if there's any reason that she doesn't want to go and the answer is that she wants to stay home or that she misses me. It seems she does it more often when I'm working night shifts; doesn't like me not being here for bedtime. Midshifts seem easier for her.

The only recurring issue regarding any other child is one on the bus who used to be in her kindergarten class ... blocking her leaving, saying things that aren't true, etc. Not observing it myself, I'm not sure what's going on. I've told April and Beckett that this child may miss them and doesn't realize that her behavior isn't the right way to go about being friends. I've also told them that all of them are still learning how to be good friends, and everyone will make mistakes sometimes.

I asked her about today. It took a while, but what I got from her was that little Bobby said "boo" to her 3 times and she was scared. I asked her why she hid under the table ... she was upset that no one noticed (not sure about the "boo" or her being gone). Tommy eventually asked her why she was sad. I suggested to her that if she was scared/sad, hiding under the table wasn't a good way to solve the problem, especially if she wanted someone to notice and that she should seek out Mrs. Jackson or yourself for help.

The talking to herself is her imaginative play. If you are able listen to her, you'll hear her have complete conversations and running narratives. I'm usually very impressed with her vocabulary. LOL! The good news is she feels comfortable/safe enough at school to have them. The bad news is that she needs to learn she can't always do it when she wants.

We've been getting more attitude from her since she cut her hair. <sigh> I've been hoping it's just because she's 7 and trying to expand her limits.

If you need to put her on a schedule to see you regularly, we're fine with that. I'm open to suggestions for things we can do at home. Except I can't change my work situation. I wish I could.
Thanks,
Vivian

From: Sunny
To: Me
Date: February 13, 2012

Hi! Thanks for your response.
I know April has not been feeling quite herself. This inconsistent

weather doesn't help anyone. My plan for April is to have some social stories on hand to help her learn how to cope with social situations, particularly those which cause her anxiety.
Thanks again!
Sunny

From: Me
To: Sunny
Date: February 13, 2012

She saw the doc this morning and she'll be on antibiotics starting tonight. Doc isn't sure they'll work, though. Seems to think it might be a stomach virus. :-(She had a fever most of the weekend.
For what it's worth, we don't observe any anxiety in social situations, but that may be because we're there. I know when she was first diagnosed with a social development delay in Pre-K that her behavior was different if we weren't around (tested it with her aunt/cousins to get a 3rd party's observation). What we do at home is when we read stories, we ask a lot of "feeling" questions ... "How do you think she feels? Why? What would make her feel better?" etc. If you have suggestions for anything else, just let me know.
Thanks!
Vivian

From: Sunny
To: Me
Date: February 13, 2012

Hi!
I think your approach with the feelings questions is great! I am thinking of using the social stories in school because I think there are times when she isn't sure about to handle certain situations that surface. For example, on Friday, I think there was a part of April that wasn't sure how to handle her fear that led to her hiding under the desk. My perspective is that she was "stuck" in the moment and did

not know how to approach the situation that would yield a successful
outcome for her. The social stories can help her develop the necessary
social tools and hopefully less emotional reactions. :-)
I'll keep you posted!
Sunny

❧

As you can see from the emails, April's teachers and I would communicate regularly if any of us thought something in April's life might create or indicate problems in the other setting, and worked together to form a complete picture and develop plans to help her cope and progress. Sadly, I have heard stories of other families not being so lucky in their school districts.

Another example: April's second grade teacher saw me in the school office one day and mentioned that April wouldn't look her in the eye when she asked and started crying. Her teacher was concerned, as she had just wanted to pay April a compliment on her work. But April had completely shut down before she had had an opportunity to do so. When I questioned April about it, April said she believed she was in trouble for something. I told her that her teacher was worried that April didn't like her anymore when all her teacher had wanted to do was see her big, beautiful blue eyes.

After I relayed my conversation to her teacher, she began asking April regularly if she could see her beautiful blue eyes so she (the teacher) could be sure that April wasn't upset with her. She then followed up with an encouraging word for her schoolwork or something positive. And that was one way we were slowly able to increase April's tolerance and comfort level for eye contact with people outside of the immediate family. Shades of ABA therapy, yes, but in April's natural everyday environment and at her own pace, without her ever feeling forced to make a change.

❧

As I mentioned before, chewing was a problem for April. At school, her support teacher would allow her gum and other chewy treats in the support classroom to attempt to reduce April's need. In fourth grade, I purchased silicone sensory necklaces meant for chewing, which helped for a little while; then she seemed to need the chewing more than she had before, so we went back to the original supports. Sometimes you try new things and they don't work as hoped. You just regroup and attempt something else.

In fourth grade, the students began to rotate regularly between three classrooms in preparation for junior high. This helped April with some of her need to move regularly, but we still needed to build in an hour break from the general education classrooms in the early afternoon. The timing of her break worked well with her class schedule in that she was able to attend the first half of her math class and learn new material, then head to the support classroom to do the remainder of the classwork in a less stressful environment before heading back to the general education classrooms for the rest of the school day.

❧

April has always had a great deal of school anxiety, not just about whether the teachers would like her (most *loved* her), but also about achieving perfection in her school work. We spent a year helping her learn that it was okay to answer questions out of order on her homework, quiz, or test and that it was actually less stressful for her to answer everything she knew well before completing the more difficult questions. As much work as that was, it was not nearly as painful as developing hypotheses in fourth grade science! She would refuse to choose one because "What if it's wrong?" Trying to get her to understand that the only wrong answer was no answer at all was exceedingly difficult. Honestly, I'm still not sure she does completely understand it.

These were the years when I learned that once April had a thought that was entrenched due to her autism's emotional reaction, there was no way to change that pathway of thought in her mind. We call it her *hamster on the wheel*, or as Sunny put it in her earlier email, "stuck in the moment." Instead we had to find ways to build alternate pathways of thought that went around, over, or under her hamster on the wheel. I became an expert at reframing issues to help her.

～

It was during these years that April began the process of noticing the people around her more. Those with autism can be very self-involved. Not from selfishness, but, I believe, because so much of their energy and focus is directed to coping with all the input. Awareness of others—faces, social situations, and cues—is rendered secondary and is therefore ignored as much as possible. It has been my experience that as someone with autism gains proficiency in handling the sensory input, their worlds start to expand outward from themselves a little at a time.

In the process of noticing her peers, April sometimes became anxious that her classmates didn't like her. Nothing could have been further from the truth. Her classmates were sometimes confused when she wouldn't play with them, but most really wanted to be her friend, because she was smart and funny. When she would have an especially rough day at school with meltdowns, I would get calls, emails, and texts from other parents telling me that their child was worried about April and wanted to know if she was okay now. I think many of her peers felt helpless because they didn't know how to help someone they liked when she was in distress.

Incidents

The following email exchange took place after we received a phone call from April's third-grade teacher that both children had been waving pencils in another child's face while in the afternoon bus line.

Note: Penny Wars is a fundraiser where coins count as positive points and bills count as negative points. In this instance, a classroom could "sabotage" a second classroom by giving a bill to the that classroom, which would increase the money raised by the second classroom, but reduce their overall points. The classroom with the most points (not money) at the end of the fundraiser would win a prize.

From: Me
To: Mrs. Johnson (April's 3rd grade teacher); Mrs. Smith (teacher responsible for bus line duty)
CC: Sunny
Date: May 28, 2014

Ladies,
John and I had a long conversation with the children about the incident today. It appears that April instigated the behavior because she didn't want Miss Trey's class to sabotage her class again in Penny Wars. While there was no real intent to harm Mary, and despite April's insistence that she really didn't mean to scare Mary, we believe that there WAS the intent to scare/bully Mary to get her own way. We explained how easily Mary could've been hurt if someone had bumped any one of them and how badly she could've been hurt. We also reinforced that bullying anyone for any reason was unacceptable and that what they chose to do was also cheating to win.

The making amends portion/owning their actions and accepting the consequences of their behavior include written apologies to both Mary and Mrs. Smith. We've told them that we expect them to deliver the letters personally and make verbal apologies as well. The letters are in their binders. Please make sure that happens and that the apologies are sincere. We also told them that it was entirely up to Mary on whether or not she would immediately forgive them, and they should not expect it, as the apologies were not about them being forgiven, but acknowledgement that what they did was wrong and about her feelings.

They have been told to expect to have their teachers speak with them about their behavior, and possibly Mrs. Brown. They have also been told that we expect them to accept whatever consequences decided by any of you without tears, since they now know how wrong they were.

The punishment portion involves:
Neither one is allowed to participate in Penny Wars for the rest of

the week. (We also explained that because of their poor behavior, there will now be less money to help Children's Hospital.) They feel this was the worst punishment of all.

They have lost all home computer/NABI privileges for one week, except for school-related activities, and even for those they must ask permission first. They are also aware that if they violate this punishment in any way, we will consider it willful disobedience on their part and the punishment will be extended for an additional two weeks.

As upset as I am that this happened, I do have to share a funny story about the discussion about punishment. We asked for their input and asked how long they should lose their privileges. April said, "I typically learn things faster than Beckett, so I think a week for me and two weeks for him." And he agreed! LOL!

Anyway, that's what's been done here. With any luck, the lesson(s) will be internalized quickly.
Thanks,
Vivian

From: Mrs. Johnson
To: Me, Mrs. Smith, Mrs. White (Beckett's 3rd grade teacher)
Cc: Sunny, Mrs. Brown (principal)
Date: May 29, 2014

Thank you, Vivian~ I was not going to keep them after school to investigate, but did feel it warranted sitting at the front of the bus. As I told you last night on the phone, I knew that you would be able to get all of the facts so that we could speak to them today. As much as I did not feel it was malicious, as they were both smiling when I saw them with the pencils, the information that you just shared makes complete sense as April has had a very hard time with others sabotaging our class. Just yesterday I had her go with me to sabotage a class to have fun and not cry. We even went to see Sunny to discuss that this should be fun. I told April that every time a child sabotaged us that we were the lucky ones who could help buy another hearing aid for a child… that seemed to work in the moment.

Thank you for your quick response and immediate consequences for both of them. We will follow up today here at school and let you know what we decide.

Take Care,

Sally

P.S. Such a typical funny moment with April's interpretation of disciplining them!!!!

From: Me
To: Mrs. Johnson, Mrs. Smith, Mrs. White
CC: Sunny, Mrs. Brown
Date: May 29, 2014

Sally,

Thanks. It did come out in the discussion that the pencils just happened to be objects of opportunity, as they were planning on doing their homework on the bus and had them out already.

Let me know how it goes.

Thanks,

Vivian

From: Mrs. White
To: Me, Mrs. Johnson, Mrs. Smith
Cc: Sunny, Mrs. Brown
Date: May 29, 2014

Vivian,

As Sally said, thank you for handling the situation so quickly. I am sure that they are unhappy with the choices that they made as well as the consequences that follow.

Talk with you soon,

Barbara

Mrs. Brown reviewed the school's security tapes, spoke with everyone involved, and asked me to come in for a meeting. She was uncertain as to what discipline to give our children, as in her words, "They are good kids who made a poor decision." Since they had received significant consequences at home, she was confident they would learn the lesson, but she still had to discipline them. After some discussion, we decided that they would miss part of the annual Field Day activities and have to write essays on what they had learned.

Mrs. Brown told me afterwards that she had sat in the room with them while they were writing their essays, counting and wrapping the change from the Penny Wars fundraiser, and that April had started to tear up. When Mrs. Brown asked if she should call me as she had my number on speed-dial, both children emphatically said, "No! Our mom is really mad at us." I recently asked them if they remembered the Penny Wars from third grade; from the tones of their *yeah*s, I believe the lessons stuck.

In second grade, April matter-of-factly told us one day that Beckett's teacher had called her a crybaby the previous week. She was not upset, just relating what had happened. It seems the entire grade had watched a movie together, and Beckett's teacher told April she couldn't sit with Beckett, so April started crying. Beckett's teacher then made a comment to the effect, "Oh, go ahead and sit with him, you crybaby."

I was concerned, confused, and unsure how to proceed. Did my daughter relay the situation to me correctly? Was there something else going on that would add better context to the story? I liked and respected all their teachers; I did not want to be *that mom*, at least not without better information at my disposal.

I found a way to unofficially learn the circumstances and discovered that Beckett's teacher was unaware of his being a twin or that April had autism and that there were some other personal worries going on in her life at that time that had affected her overall patience level at the end of a long week. The teacher apologized to both children without me ever speaking to her or her superiors. I made it a point every year afterwards to email all their teachers a joint email to try to ensure there wouldn't be a similar situation in the future.

Socialization & Outings

From the time they were little, we would have birthday parties at home for Beckett and April with friends and family. Often, I overdid my preparations, would have a theme most years, and became known to some of their classmates as the mom who threw really cool parties. For their toddler parties, I would make special cakes; I think their favorites were the Rocket character from Little Einsteins, French fries, and pink puppy-dog cakes. I believe their favorite pinata was Dr. Doofenshmirtz from the Phineas and Ferb cartoon.

A little over a year after the hospitalization mentioned in the previous email, I became ill again. Unfortunately, it was at a time when I had a lot going on. I had been able to obtain a doctor's appointment for the Friday afternoon, which was the same day I had to set up Santa's Workshop. It was also the weekend of the twins' birthday party. I woke up at three o'clock on Friday morning to bake and decorate cookies for the kids' classes—I think that year was Power Rangers, for which I was going to try to use a black sugar topping. John got up as well and told me to sit and just instruct him what to do. Between the two of us, we got the cookies done, but they looked horrendous—a true Pinterest fail. I was too sick to even cry about it. I just put the cookies in their baggies and went back to sleep for a bit.

John was worried I was going to be hospitalized again and took the day off from work to come help set up Santa's Workshop, make certain I didn't overtax myself (although just getting out of bed was taxing enough), and drive me to the doctor's office. Fortunately, I had a lot of good volunteers that year and gave general marching orders with which they then did a wonderful job after I left. While the doctor didn't end up hospitalizing me, I still had a birthday party on the Sunday.

I spent as much time as possible in bed, letting the medications work their magic, before dragging myself out of bed to get ready for the party. I suddenly realized that I had been so ill all week, I had completely forgotten to plan a craft activity. Inspiration struck when I looked at a three-foot high Christmas tree we had on the buffet in the dining room. I had John help me gather all sorts of craft materials from around the house, including glitter.

When it came time, I told the all the children present that they were to make Christmas ornaments for the tree and for themselves to take home. Each ornament had to have a Christmas wish on the back. One caveat: They could not wish for anything for themselves, only others. Everyone stayed happily occupied while I tried to stay awake. A couple of the kids present that day have since approached me, years later, to tell me that they remember the activity with fondness. I was just trying to survive the day.

The birthday party that finally had me saying, "no more," was the Skylanders one, where I sent partygoers on a quest around our home to find various games, treats, and party favors using scrolls with poems. I had rolled over 100 tiny scrolls and had cramped fingers.

Now we have small celebrations at home or in a restaurant, just the four of us. Originally, I wanted them to have the memories of me taking the time and effort to do something memorable for them instead of renting a party facility, but as we became more aware of April's challenges, home parties really were the best environment for her to relax and enjoy her own birthday celebrations.

As a surprise birthday gift when they were seven years old, we took Beckett and April to see a Disney's *Phineas and Ferb* live production. They were entranced by it all, but my favorite memory was when the actors came into the audience. As the Perry the Platypus character passed by our row, April put a hand over her heart, smiled, and swooned. Yes, swooned.

⁓

Being such close siblings, our children have always been very good about sharing. Beckett, especially, likes to have everyone around him happy and feeling good about themselves. He was the child who would stop in the middle of a soccer field to congratulate a child on the opposing team on a goal or good try. Which was why it was surprising to us when his first grade teacher told us he would get upset if other children took things from his desk. We found out that it wasn't that he minded sharing with any of his classmates, he just wanted them to ask first.

∽

Each summer, we would enroll Beckett and April for three 2-week-long day camps at a local YMCA. April would have some issues occasionally, but having Beckett with her, they did not happen nearly as often as they might have if she'd been alone.

∽

At our district's elementary schools, the various PTAs plan a celebration for the graduating fourth graders before they move on to junior high (for fifth to eighth grade). The year our children were leaving their elementary school, our PTA rented a pool area in a nearby housing plan, complete with DJ, games, photo booth, and food. I had arranged with the photo booth vendor to receive digital copies of all the photos taken to use in a memory book for our fourth grade students. I was surprised but also delighted to see April's happy face in so many photos, as she had decided to enjoy herself photobombing her classmates and teachers. My guess is that it was a way for her to participate in the fun without having to worry about a lot of social interaction or conversation.

While I have many fond memories of that day, there is one that is not so cheerful that stands out clearly in my mind. April was in the pool, standing off to the side by herself, watching her classmates play various games in the water or on floats. She had an intense, sad look on her face, studying her classmates closely, wanting to join the fun but unsure as to how to do so. My heart broke for my little girl's pain.

CHAPTER 10

EXPLAINING THE DIAGNOSIS

We're all different, with different color eyes that see

We're all the same, we all have a heart that beats

We're all different, with different hair color and smiles

We're all the same, we all love to laugh and sometimes cry

Hold hands together and celebrate

We're all different and we're the same

— "We're all Different and We're the Same"

THE FOLLOWING EMAIL exchange took place during April's fourth-grade year.

From: Sunny (April's Support Teacher)
To: Me
Date: January 26, 2015

Hi Vivian,
I apologize for not responding to you sooner. (I was out sick several days last week.)

I have a few suggestions to offer that may help alleviate some of April's anxiety and hopefully increase her self-esteem.

As you know, April is very intelligent and as you mentioned in your email perceives herself as "different." With that in mind, it may not be a bad idea to begin dialogue about her diagnosis. I have a few books and resources that you could use with her that can help facilitate the conversation and ultimately help April come to the realization that different *doesn't mean* less or not good enough. *If she is able to comprehend her diagnosis over time, then she may have the chance to like herself.*

Let me know what you think about this. Of course, I would be willing to support you in any way possible if this is the direction you would choose to take.

I also think it would be beneficial to have her meet with our guidance counselor on a routine basis to help her with her self-esteem. I will continue to meet with April on a regular basis as well. Please let me know if there is anything else I can do to help.
Sunny

From: Me
To: Sunny
Date: January 27, 2015

Sunny,
I spoke with John about it and we think explaining to April with the books/resources is a good idea. She's old enough now and definitely smart enough to start having the discussions in an age-appropriate way. If there are any particular books, etc., you think would be help-ful for me to buy and have here for the future, just let me know what they are and I'll get them. I've read other books with her through the years about people being different and how different is okay and have tried numerous times to lead her to realize that everyone is different and that's what makes it fun and interesting, to no real avail.

I have no problems with April seeing the guidance counselor for additional support for her self-esteem.

Just a few things that have popped up here in the last week or two:

She's been saying she thinks she's "cursed" because people don't allow her to do what she wants to do when she wants to do it. This usually occurs when I say no more computer/TV/video games or when it's time to do homework or go to bed.

I apologized to her for her Lumbard genes. I had a discussion with her how all of us have a tendency to be "noticed" and have all had to learn to be comfortable with it. If you knew my family, you'd understand the meaning of eccentric and flamboyant. I'm the most normal one of the bunch. My husband calls me a catalyst. LOL!
I hope you're feeling better!
Vivian

From: Sunny
To: Me
Date: January 27, 2015

Hi Vivian,
I have a few books and I will compile some more information for you as well. Let me know when you are ready for them and I will have them in the office for you.
Again, anything I can do to support you, I'll be happy to help!
Sunny

From: Me
To: Sunny
Date: January 27, 2015

Sunny,
Any time in the next couple days is fine. I'll be in and out picking up/ dropping off PTA stuff.
Thanks,
Vivian

From: Me
To: Sunny
Cc: Mrs. Taylor (April's guidance counselor)
Date: January 27, 2015

Sunny,
We began discussions tonight with April about her diagnosis (well,
I did most of the talking with John chiming in here and there. :-)).
I've cc'd her guidance counselor since she'll be providing additional
support for April and I think it's best if you both know how the topic
was explained to her so we're all giving her consistent information (or
at least not contradicting each other) if she chooses to bring it up with
either of you.

I started out with telling her that I wanted to talk about how
sometimes she feels she doesn't fit in and how it makes her sad and
explain why that was. I explained the concept of a spectrum (broad
range) and a very general overview of autistic spectrum. I, at no time,
used the words diagnosis *or* disorder *when talking to her; I didn't*
want to take the chance that she might latch onto one of those words
at this early stage and think she was sick or something was wrong
with her. I told her that people at the low end of the spectrum had
more challenges to meet more often, while those at the higher end
might not have as many challenges to cope with regularly. I told her
that those at the low end of the spectrum sometimes couldn't even hug
their parents, not because they didn't want to, but because it some-
times feels like it physically hurts them to touch other people.

I told her that Asperger's was at the higher end and she was just
above that so some of the Asperger challenges were hers as well, but
not all of them and some not as often.

I told her that no one was really sure yet why some people were
on the spectrum, but that it was no different than Beckett having
one eye so strong that he needed glasses to train it to stay straight or
Daddy being born with blue eyes, it's just how some people are born.
I reminded her of when we were having Beckett tested for possible

absence seizures last year and how we thought some of his brain cells were so loud and rowdy that the others forgot to do what they were supposed to for a few seconds. I told her that I thought what was happening was her brain cells were sometimes competing with each other (one says, "I see a bird," while others say, "but I see trains; I hear this noise; I see this color," etc.) and when too many of them do that all at once, she can't keep up with all of them or sort them out right away and it creates stress and causes her to lose focus.

I told her the story about how there was a brief time when she was a baby that she didn't want to cuddle and I worried that she might grow up thinking I didn't love her as much as her brother because I gave him more hugs and kisses and that simply wasn't true. But then not long afterwards she wanted to cuddle, so I didn't need to worry about that anymore. (Awww, sweet girl moment when she immediately launched herself into my arms to give me a hug after hearing the story.)

I reminded her of how far she has come in the last 6 years and that we knew sometimes it was very difficult for her, but we were extremely proud of how much better she is at recognizing when things are getting too much and communicating it. I told her that Mommy and Daddy didn't always get it completely right, but we were trying our best to make sure she has everything she needs (not necessarily what she wants) to keep getting better at it so she didn't have to feel as stressed.

I told her that pretty much everyone has at least one trait on the autistic spectrum, but it is easier to cope with when it was only one or two, so no one really notices it. I also told her that growing up is difficult at times for everyone, especially during puberty, and most kids worry about fitting in, being different, or if people really like them, etc., then. I told her she might have an easier time by that point because she has been getting support and learning how to "feel" different before many of her friends/classmates.

I told her that *everyone* was different and wouldn't it be boring if everyone were the same? There would be no one to think of some-

thing new, like Angry Birds, an invention, or make us think to try a new activity.

I also told her that there were a lot of people (grownups and kids) who didn't understand what it was like to be on the spectrum and sometimes might say hurtful things, but we wanted her to understand it was not her fault and she would get better coping when that may happen in the future as long as she talked to us or her teachers. (Good news, no reports from her of bullying, etc., from her classmates!)

We read the All Cats Have Asperger's Syndrome book together as a family with each of us "owning" different traits—that sounds like Mommy, etc. It was helpful to see where she felt an immediate connection and where she just said, "That's not me." I've ordered copies of both books you sent home (and a couple others, too) for us to have here and read/discuss whenever she wants.

She brought up how she was worried about going to the junior high next year and how much she was going to miss you, Sunny. I told her that I had heard that the autistic support teacher at the junior high was really nice, too, and she would be visiting the junior high before the end of this school year. I told her that if she was still feeling uncomfortable after that, all she had to do was tell me and I would arrange for her to spend some more time there with the teacher to make it seem less worrisome for her. I could see her shoulders relax when I made that promise to her. She really is very worried about that transition.

I used words like challenge, cope, handle, recognize, *and* communicate, *and avoided ones like* overcome, get over/past, wrong, normal, *or anything like that and overall, kept it very matter of fact except during the book reading, where it was more a fun family activity. I didn't really hit on the social challenges so much during this initial discussion; I thought it was best to wait on that until we started reading the other material you provided since it seemed like a good jumping off point.*

My plan is to read bits of the photocopied resource material you gave me over the next couple days on my days off (I'll let her set the

pace on how much/little we read at a time), then break from the subject during my work week unless she chooses to bring it up. And we'll
do a little reading on my days off or when I'm home nights depending
on how she's reacting. I'm going to let her pretty much set the pace
after this weekend so I don't overwhelm her or give her the impression
that it's an *issue*. I'm not sure how she'll process it all or if she'll even
want to discuss it more unless I bring it up ... we'll just have to wait
and see.

She handled the discussion very well and was engaged the entire
time, but, Sunny, you may want to give her paraprofessionals a heads
up that if she starts saying things like "I think my brain cells are competing with each other," it means she's starting to get stressed. LOL!
You just never know what she'll start to share or when. :-)

If, during any of your discussions with her, there is something else
that either of you think it would be helpful for us to follow up on at
home, please let me know.

Sunny, thanks for suggesting this. I'm embarrassed to admit that
it hadn't even occurred to me to explain her diagnosis to her since
we've been living with it for so long, it didn't even register in my mind
that we had never told her more details as she got older. I do think
this will help her, not only short-term, but long-term.
Thanks,
Vivian

From: Sunny
To: Me
Date: January 29, 2015

Hi Vivian,
Thanks so much for the information. I will be sure to support her and
use the correct words when communicating with April. I think the
way you handled this was perfect. Different doesn't ever mean less!!
The Autism Speaks website has great resources for parents as does The
Watson Institute.

I know that she is nervous about next year; she will have the opportunity to meet her new support teacher (who is wonderful) and spend the day in her class as well. I know my heart will ache when April leaves us—I always cry the last day of school! She will do great at the junior high.

Her guidance counselor also plans to meet with April on Wednesdays.

Also—is it ok if we allow April to earn to have her fingernails painted? She requested rainbow colors! Just want to make sure you are ok with it!
Sunny

⤳

You may have picked up on the fact that John and I mistakenly explained April's autism to her as if it were on a scale or graph and not a spectrum. We better understand the difference now. When we think of a scale or graph, most of us might picture a horizontal or vertical line with little tick marks numbered 1-10. However, a graph implies that one position on the scale is more or less than another number, leading us to believe that the effects of autism are more or less depending on one's position on the line, which is not accurate.

I think of the spectrum like a visual depiction of seven distinct areas of sound (say bass, treble, vibrato, etc.), where those seven distinct areas cause difficulties for autistic people. Person number one might have significant challenges with information processing, so his/her soundwave for that area would be a high peak, while person number two also has information processing challenges, but not quite so much as person number one, so his/her soundwave in that area would be a little lower. In this instance, the scale/graph concept works because you are comparing one distinct area of difficulty.

It is only when we put all seven areas together with their distinct soundwaves meshed that we begin to appreciate the uniqueness of each autistic individual's music. The segments can change from moment to moment as stressors in one area occur or dissipate, so the soundwaves flex and change shape as they react to increased tempos or novel sound qualities, etc., but are all within the spectrum of the music... or ASD.

The decision to tell a child about their ASD diagnosis and when to have that discussion is a personal one for parents. Some may feel their child may not have the mental capacity to understand or is not emotionally mature enough yet; others feel that the label *autism* is not one their child should have to bear. I am sure there are a number of other factors each family considers before making their own decision. There are resources available online that enumerate more of these factors if you are not sure of whether, how, or when to share your child's diagnosis with him/her.

While it had to be suggested to us to tell April about her autism since we were wrapped up in the day-to-day, for John and me, it was an easy decision to make. April was already suffering from self-esteem issues, because she was intelligent and aware enough to know that she was somehow different from her peers, but did not understand why or how, leading her to believe there was something intrinsically wrong with her—which was and continues to be untrue.

Her self-esteem issues did not disappear overnight afterwards, but it became easier and easier for her to become more self-aware with our help. For years, she would make statements like, "I think it's my autism that makes me..." and we would be honest with her when it was her autism and when it was typical childhood behavior—really, most children would rather play than do homework or chores. I believe the way we chose to handle it enabled her to better understand how her autism affects *her*, but also reinforced that she was also the same as her peers in many other areas. By better understanding how autism affects her, she is also obtaining a better idea of what accommodations would be reasonable to expect in the future.

We included Beckett in our discussions so he would have a better understanding too. After reading *All Cats Have Asperger's Syndrome* together, we would say that when they were in womb and found out that April was going to have autism, Beckett probably decided to take

CHAPTER 11

THE MIDDLE SCHOOL/ JUNIOR HIGH YEARS

Your world is growing,

Expanding week by week.

Know that we are here

Whatever path you seek.

LOOKING BACK, I can see that April's elementary school years were a period of great growth overall as she learned to cope with many of the sensory overload issues that are commonly experienced by autistic people. By the end of fourth grade, she no longer threw herself to the floor crying regularly. Her need for chewing lessened with the substitutes we provided. She started to recognize beforehand when she was about to have a meltdown, even if she could not prevent or explain it. Her junior high school years continued that growth, but now we also saw growth in her social awareness skills.

᠅

Hope was another wonderfully supportive teacher for April... and myself. Like Sunny, she communicated with me often and genuinely cared about

April's progress. One of the changes we made to April's IEP for junior high was to have a paraprofessional in the room during general education classes for additional support because Sunny believed that April would have fewer meltdowns with someone available to aid her all day.

Early in fifth grade, Hope suggested that we withdraw April from Honors Language Arts for two reasons. One was that the classroom was heavily decorated and that the visual stimuli was creating focus problems for April. The other was that there were more writing assignments, and for a very long time, we all had difficulty finding the best ways to encourage April to start writing.

It was still early on in my relationship with Hope, and I admit I was not yet at the point of blind faith in her assessments. I went back to April's elementary school and spoke with Sunny and Mrs. Brown for their input and both supported the idea. I saw her new Academic Language Arts teacher in the hall one day, and we talked about April's fidgeting. The teacher told me she didn't care if her students needed to learn while hanging upside down, so long as they learned and understood the material. That change ended up being a very good one for April.

Manifestations

In our school district, three elementary schools' fourth grade students transition into a single junior high school's fifth grade students. April was very scared about changing schools and the fact that there would be many more students. She was able to tour the junior high with her classmates beforehand, spend a day with her new support teacher, and again tour the school a couple weeks before the school year started. At the start of the subsequent school years, we were still dealing with her tears, but we were down to a week of anxiety and crying, rather than weeks. April did not cry at all before starting eighth grade or high school.

Nose picking was a bad habit for both children, and April had a habit of putting her hand down the front of her pants at inappropriate times. I now make a point of checking what material her underwear is made from.

I purchased Vibes earplugs for April, to reduce the volume of noise input in gym class or wherever else she felt it necessary. They did work, but she'd rarely remember to use them or she'd lose them. MP3 players worked as well, but she was only allowed to use them in her support classroom or on designated iPod days at school. She relied on her MP3 player heavily at home, so much so that we had to create a rule that if we were out in public, she had to have one earbud out for safety. We needed to be certain that she would hear us (or anyone else) if she needed to be warned of, say, traffic when crossing the street.

Many of April's meltdowns at home regarding her school work, especially if they involved writing, could last one to two hours before she would be calm enough to start. It was exhausting at times for both her and me. However, at family gatherings and parties, she began to start letting me know she would need to leave soon when it was becoming too much for her. We were able to avoid many long meltdowns as her ability to sense and articulate her rising stress in those situations grew.

Playing Detective & Outings

After meltdowns, we started emphasizing to April that it was time for her to play detective, to try to understand what had made her feel stressed. She wasn't always able to articulate it, but her awareness started to grow. We began to hear her say things like: I needed help with a problem, but didn't know how to ask. The lights were confusing. The noise echoes in the gym. Over time, we all gained a better understanding of what might create issues and would brainstorm about potential problems and solutions before an event whenever possible.

We became much better at this after one summer vacation, during which we visited a Ripley's Believe It or Not. We were already aware that loud, echoey, or jumbled noises lowered April's ability to cope. It was steaming hot; in fact, earlier in the day, the beach sand had been hot enough that our feet felt like they were getting burned even with shoes on. April referred to that beach as Devil's Beach for over a year.

Our family meandered along the beach boardwalk, had something to eat at one of the food establishments, and ended up at Ripley's where we waited in line to purchase tickets. Night had fallen and the multicolored lights were flashing rapidly in no discernible order.

When inside, their aunt, who was ahead of us, called for our kids to come see something, a very large circular spinning optical illusion. April came running back to me making the barking noise she usually makes before vomiting. She and I rushed through the warren of Ripley's, searching for a trashcan, restroom, or exit. No luck, and soon, I was catching most of the contents of April's stomach in my hands. Now, poor April was mortified and crying as we finally found a way out and headed to the public restrooms to clean up.

Our post mortem of the event determined that the heat, flashing lights, and jumbled noise were all factors in her senses overloading. She had been able to cope long enough for us to get inside the air-conditioned space, which was normally lit and quieter, but the optical illusion sent her bodily senses out of control immediately. The next time we visited the area a couple years later, we tried Ripley's again so that April could learn that she was able to handle being there so long as we took precautions, such as having a bag available in the event she felt ill again. Our girl hid her eyes and averted her head as we passed by the optical illusion muttering, "I am sooo not looking at that thing again."

◄⑤►

A few months after the first visit to Ripley's, a local science museum had a laser light performance featuring the music of Queen. Knowing what had happened on vacation, none of us were sure if April would be able to cope. She and I made plans before we went for what we would do if the laser lights and music were too much for her. First, we would make sure that we were sitting somewhere where we could exit the space quickly. Second, she would wear her scarf and if she started to feel ill, we would cover her eyes with it to see if that made her feel better. If not, we would leave quickly and head to a restroom. Sadly, her senses reacted immediately to the laser lights, and she and I exited within the first minute of the performance.

John and Beckett also came out to check on April, and we girls told them we would go to the car and wait for them there so they could stay for the rest of the performance. John was worried and wanted to get April home. This was one of the only times that Beckett has ever expressed disappointment that he was missing out on something he wanted to do because of April's autism. John took Beckett to the next day's performance alone.

So, now April is aware that laser lights, strobe lights, and optical illusions are a no-go for her unless she has a carefully planned exit strategy beforehand. The good news is that John and I will never have to worry about her being a party girl in dance clubs. The bad news is that she may never be able to attend a rock concert or any performance that may have any of those sensory stressors.

One of our local theaters put on an autism-friendly performance of *Wicked*, which we attended as a family. There were people of all sorts there on the spectrum: from toddlers to seniors, from individuals in wheelchairs to the ambulatory, the non-verbal and the verbal, those who needed service animals and those who didn't. What wasn't there: judgmental looks from other theater goers, impatience or uneducated or uninformed comments. Entire families could relax knowing that if their loved one showed they needed a break, by whatever means they could manage, *everyone* there understood. It was evident that a great deal of thought and understanding had gone into the planning by the number and variety of choices of supports put in place in case anyone needed them. I now look for other autism-friendly performances for us to attend.

Interests & Socialization

Beckett decided he wanted to play the trumpet in the general band and the jazz band. He enjoyed himself, but rarely brought his trumpet home to practice. I doubt I heard him play the instrument at home more than a dozen times in four years. But he had shown some innate ability playing by ear on our piano and electric organ.

☙

April and Beckett joined the after-school art club as well as the comic book club during their first year of junior high. They added the video announcements club to the list the following year. Neither had many friends they wanted to interact with outside of school, but we started to hear more stories about peers at home.

☙

Beckett and April's interest in video games grew and April became quite proficient at Splatoon, Tetris, and Puyo Puyo. We began to hear them use the words *murder* and *suicide* talking about their game characters while playing. John and I would tell them that we didn't want them using those words in that context, since words have power. Murder and suicide are serious, powerful words and should never be spoken lightly.

Pokemon had been an earlier obsession for both, and they began to ask to attend Pokemon pre-release tournaments. Building from these interests, April also developed an interest in Japan; she would like to visit the country in the future and has even begun using the internet to try to learn the language on her own.

They continued attending the YMCA summer camps, and we were able to afford a one-week ID Tech computer camp two summers in a row, as well as a couple camps at an arts center for digital animation. Their animation instructor pulled me aside at the end of the camp and suggested that I invest in Wacom tablets for both children and encourage them to continue with their interests, as both, but especially Beckett, were far ahead of most children their age. Both choose to draw digitally often, and we are proud of the progress we continue to see in their finished works. April, in particular, is beginning to depict emotion in her characters simply with body language.

☙

Beckett had lobbied for a cell phone for years. Each time he asked, we told him that they were never anywhere where there wasn't a responsible adult with them with a cell phone, so they had no need for one. Long before they received cell phones, John and I spent a lot of time going over our expectations, rules, and what they should do if they came across disturbing content, either on the web or sent to them by anyone. One of those rules was that any future phone needed to be charged downstairs and was not allowed in their bedrooms at night. Our reasoning was that a phone was a way to let the outside world into their lives and the world should not have access to them 24-7. Another rule, piggybacking on our electronic games rule, was that as soon as food was served at a meal, cell phones were put away. We explained EXIF (Exchangeable Image File) data, and how their locations could be found with a photo. We didn't allow them their own cell phones until the summer before they turned fourteen years old. And when they do get laptops in the future, the same rules will apply.

While our decision to delay cell phones was primarily based on keeping them relatively safe until we felt they had enough maturity to understand and follow the rules and also to allow for increased time interacting with people face-to-face, it did have another unexpected and completely welcome result. Beckett and April had the opportunity to observe some situations at school where social media, cyberbullying, and online feuds were involved. They saw the drama, and it has made them even more cautious with what they post online and has positively affected their choices on who they allow to have their phone numbers.

John and I had noticed that Beckett and April had naturally gravitated to friendships with other children on the spectrum or close to it. We have liked all of their school friends with the exception of one Beckett had early on in elementary school. Our dislike of that friendship had nothing to do with that child's special needs but everything to do with his/her attitude towards others. Beckett drifted away from that friendship on his own before junior high. We are happy that Beckett and April have been choosing friendships with genuinely nice, kind children.

One day in eighth grade, April came home and said she didn't know what to do. She felt her Physical Education classmates were trying to help her keep her stress levels down by not passing her the ball during one particular game because, she suspected, they knew she might have difficulties. Yet, she also felt that the participation portion of her grade was suffering because, to the teacher, it looked like April wasn't trying. We discussed her options. She elected not to tell the teacher, because she felt her classmates were attempting to be nice to her. This didn't help her grade, but she was more concerned that her classmates might get into trouble. Unfortunately, April did not feel comfortable talking to her classmates about the situation either. We respected her decision and told her that so long as she passed Physical Education, we would not intervene.

John had participated in stage crew in high school and college, so we tried encouraging our children to help with the musical productions too. We were unsuccessful in convincing the kids to try it, which is a shame. They loved attending the musical productions, as well as the teacher involved, and it would have been a great activity for them to share with their father during their teenage years. Maybe they will change their minds in high school.

Education

Our school district began introducing flexible seating and some other innovations in some classrooms. While I felt that flexible seating might help April at times with her fidgeting, I kept a close eye on whether the loosened structure was creating additional stress for her. I passed along my concerns to the school district administration that they needed to ensure that with these changes, they did not leave the students who require more structure behind, whether those students were autistic or neurotypical.

Our district also began a greater push toward more group work, not just in the STEAM (science, technology, engineering, arts, and mathematics) classrooms, but in the general classroom environments. I agreed that being able to work in a group is an important skill for the students' futures but again cautioned the administration that clearly defined roles for each member of a group should be taught to the students and reiterated for each assignment. There are students who require more structure and, as in April's case, who has a fear of working with people she doesn't know well, the students should be aware of individual expectations.

I always filled out the school district questionnaires annually on what I felt was working or not working as it pertained to the special education department. One year, I suggested that the general education teachers should receive more training on what types of supports are common for various special needs, as well as why they were important. Our district began implementing my suggestion not long afterwards.

During my research, I noted a larger push nationwide for social and emotional learning (SEL) in our schools for all students. With the rise of the use of electronic devices by children at younger ages, children aren't learning social skills through play as they did in generations past, so now educators are seeing more behaviors in neurotypical children that resemble the autistic traits of high emotional reactivity and social awareness challenges. Some proponents want SEL for the higher test scores and improved behaviors; others want it to aid children dealing with trauma. I would like to see it because it can only help all our children, neurotypical and autistic alike.

By now, the school district was also considering test scores during class placement, which meant that Beckett and April would have some classes together. Beckett was assigned to a fast track for mathematics courses; in essence, he would be a year ahead in the subject than many of their peers. Both were in many honors classes and overall, did well with the increased difficulty.

At some point, we discovered that April was becoming resistant to using her Break card, even when it was clear she needed it. We were able to determine that it was because she didn't want to miss class time, thereby missing important content and potentially falling behind. After more discussion, we also discovered that many of the instances in which April thought she needed a break were not for sensory reasons, but rather that she needed help with the work. This was one of the first instances where I worked with April to find a school solution that she thought would work for her and that she would be comfortable utilizing. After our discussion, we had Hope create a Help card, and things became a little easier for everyone.

❧

April had all of her club advisors as teachers at some point during her time in junior high. There were a couple that went above and beyond with both our children. We were contacted by them to let us know that Beckett's video production abilities were well above his peers and that we should encourage him to continue. They were also able to encourage April over the years to the point where she felt comfortable appearing in front of the camera with her brother and Torchic—whom you'll meet in the next chapter—for some of the school's morning announcements.

One of those teachers had April for Language Arts. He once told me that, during a lesson, he had asked the class what a certain passage meant. He said April raised her hand (even while her head was down on her desk and she was fidgeting in her unique way) and answered the question correctly. He told me that his thought then had been, "Great. Now what am I going to teach for the next 20 minutes?" because April had made the analysis and mental leap in a few moments. I credit this teacher for making the most progress increasing her comfort level with creative writing, while her teacher in eighth grade in the same subject did a wonderful job working with her to increase her comfort level debating topics with her peers in small groups.

Self-Esteem

The annual suicide awareness and prevention assemblies at school upset April. Each time, our concerns on her mental state would rise sharply, and we would become hyperaware of her emotions. Her distress was an empathetic one; she was sad that others didn't get the help they needed and that the discussions had to happen. Every year we would be asked if we wanted to excuse her from the assemblies; every year we said no. Our thinking was it was a good barometer for us to judge her feelings as we had discussions with her afterwards, which gave us meaningful opportunities to reiterate the importance of talking about the subject, especially if someone were contemplating the act.

Discussions about her future started to cause her to melt down to the point that she could not speak. Each time there was an assignment about what she thought she might like to do after high school, I would spend hours assuring her that what she thinks she might like now does not mean that is what she has to do. John and I would remind her that both he and I had started college in majors that differed from the careers we ended up choosing. She would make comments about how she was going to live with me forever. I would reiterate that while we had no intentions of making her move out right after high school, there was going to come a time when she would naturally want to have her own space where she could make the rules. A number of times she would tell me she didn't want to grow up, and I would tell her none of us have a choice in the matter; it simply happens all on its own.

We were having more discussions about April's negative self-talk tendencies when her hamster on the wheel would be telling her she was an idiot, stupid, etc. When she was calm, I would ask if she would think another classmate was stupid if he or she had answered a question wrong in class. No. Would she call another student an idiot if he or she made a mistake? No. I would then ask her why she thought it was okay to talk to herself in a way that she would never talk to another human being. No answer.

I explained that all of us, especially girls, would sometimes be negative in our thinking towards ourselves, but that her autism magnified it because her brain was getting stuck and not moving to where she could remember that everyone makes mistakes, and that she is always still learning. I relayed to her what I used to tell my work trainees, "Mistakes will happen. The trick is to recognize them before something bad happens; fix them; learn from them; and move on." Then I would remind her to try to remember to talk to herself the same way she talks to others, and I did not like anyone, including her, badmouthing my daughter.

Health

April would rush through brushing her teeth, and I ended up purchasing three-sided toothbrushes for her to use to improve her dental health. Beckett had a small gap between his front teeth that would benefit from braces, but it wasn't truly necessary to fix it. April, on the other hand, had two incisors that grew in high in her mouth, had bite issues, and crowding of her teeth. We were concerned that it was her teeth that were causing her to sound as if she were mumbling at times, rather than her autism.

Despite April's protests that she did not want braces, I took her to get them in eighth grade. She did exceptionally well in the chair, but when she saw the braces in the mirror, a slow silent tear ran down her face and she shot a look at me that should have incinerated me on the spot. She refused to speak to me.

Knowing her mouth had to be sore, I offered a chocolate milkshake and French fries. That seemed to perk her up, and she decided I was worth speaking to again. We got home, she took one bite of a French fry, and a bracket fell off. Uh, geez. I have to go back and admit I gave her French fries first thing? Maybe that could wait until tomorrow. Before she was done eating, another had fallen off, and I had no choice but to get her back to the orthodontist right away.

It seemed the bite problems we were trying to correct had caused the brackets to fall off with the added pressure of food between the teeth. They shifted a couple brackets, built up some molars, and we were good to go. April has been very good about wearing her bands; I think I've only had to remind her twice in all this time. I believe she wants the braces off as soon as possible. It has been about a year, and I can see the difference in her face as her teeth have moved closer to their proper position and her speech is much clearer now. Some of that may be increased confidence in coping with her autism too, but the braces have definitely helped. Now her smile more closely matches her personality.

Slowly Maturing

As the children grew older and more responsible, John and I began planning the transition to allowing them to stay home alone on occasion. After getting Beckett and April's input on their comfort levels, we would leave them alone for short periods during daylight hours when we expected to be only a few minutes from home and could return immediately if needed. Trips to the bank and the post office to start, and then longer periods at the grocery store before I started planning for them to come home to an empty house after school. Every couple of weeks, I would tell them that I would not be there when they got home and they would have to call John or me to let us know they had arrived safely.

Occasionally, we would take one child or the other with us on an errand, so the other could be home by themselves. If we had plans to go out at night for a few hours, we would ask the children if they wanted to stay home alone or have my mother come stay with them. The first few times, they wanted Grandma, but eventually were comfortable with being home alone at night so long as we were home by bedtime.

Easter weekend 2019, John wasn't feeling well. On Sunday afternoon, I packed up the kids and we went to their aunt's home for dinner while John stayed in bed. After a couple hours, I received a call from John asking me to come home and take him to the hospital. We left the kids home while John and I went to the emergency room, where he was eventually diagnosed with acute pancreatitis. He needed to be transferred to a Pittsburgh hospital, but a bed would not be opening up there until the middle of the night.

I drove home to pack John a bag and informed Beckett and April what was happening. I asked if they wanted to return with me to wait all night or stay home alone. They chose to stay home alone. It was a scary night for me. Not only was John seriously ill, but the kids were staying home alone overnight for the first time without us preplanning it, and at a time when I couldn't get back to them immediately if something went wrong. Our children did great, and for the next week, they did everything I asked of them without complaint or delay while John was in the hospital. Thankfully, John's illness took place after we had already laid the groundwork ensuring they were comfortable home alone.

⤳

John and I had refrained from discussing politics in our home around our kids for many years for two reasons. One, we wanted our children to experience the innocence of childhood for as long as possible, and two, we wanted to raise critical thinkers. We did not need our children to parrot our political views but instead wanted them to develop their own political belief systems based on our family's most important life values: being kind and accepting of others, showing compassion, and a number of other values. Once the children started sharing their views on the 2016 presidential election, John and I would ask questions of them to aid in clarifying their thoughts and sometimes play devil's advocate to encourage their independent analyses. But we still refrained from sharing our opinions.

After the results of the election were in, April was in tears and indignant. "Now people are going think it's okay to discriminate against me because I am a girl **and** have autism." It took us some time to calm her down, reminding her that good people that treat others fairly were still around and that those people would not change their normal behavior based on the results of an election.

Family Traditions

Our morning bus routine ritual began to morph. "Have a great day" became "Have a great wonderful day." April would not always want a hug and kiss. Sometimes, her body language would suggest the kiss should be on her forehead or nose instead. By the end of these years, Beckett would be presenting his cheek to me for a kiss, and while hugs for us were not as prevalent in public, they were always available at home.

John and I also started a family tradition that probably sounds odd to outsiders. Given Beckett's propensity to cavort around the house when he was happy or excited, we started saying things like, "Are you being happy *again?*" or "I don't remember giving you permission to be happy," or "There he goes being happy again." When April does something that indicates she is happy, we do the same with her. Both children know we are teasing and will sometimes reply with something to the effect of "You don't get to choose whether or not I'm happy."

Beyond the fact that they are getting some reinforcement in owning their own emotions, I like the tradition for another reason. With any luck, when they look back on these years and tell the story of how often we joked with each about their happiness in the moment, they will realize that they truly were happy a lot of the time. That's what I hope they remember most.

Our nighttime routines changed to my spending a few minutes with each child in their respective rooms, lying next to them. Sometimes we would discuss their day or an event or engage in one of our family's silly I-love-you traditions. Many times, this is when I discovered that something was bothering them, and they would want to share their thoughts in the dark with no one else listening.

Retirement

As a federal air traffic controller, I had enough time in service that I was eligible to retire at fifty years old and would be required to retire by the age of fifty-six if I was still talking to airplanes. About a year before I was eligible, I began discussions with John about my retirement because I wanted to retire at the earliest possible moment. I had not been able to stay home with the kids for very long when they were young, and I felt it was important to be home during the teenage years for them. Furthermore, my chronic back issues had gotten to the point that, some days, I couldn't climb the stairs to the control tower more than once a shift and would have to request an accommodation to stay in the radar room. And I was no longer feeling challenged or even needed in my workplace.

John was resistant to the idea as he wasn't sure about the financial ramifications to the family and was concerned that I, with my Type AAA personality, would become bored. I was finally able to convince him that we would be financially fine overall and I had so many interests and potential projects that I still would not be able to complete them all in my lifetime. I retired about a month before my fifty-first birthday. Not long afterwards, I began receiving emails from April's teachers: "Has something changed at home? April is much more relaxed than she has been."

Even though we had clearly communicated my schedule to the children daily, April had been carrying stress about the irregularity of the schedule. We didn't realize how much it had affected her until the stressor was removed. Once she knew I would be there every night, she was able to release all that worry and use that energy towards coping with her other challenges. I only wish I had retired sooner.

Another benefit to my retirement was that we were able to start having family dinners together regularly. About 50% of the time, April will remain at the table after dinner and have a short conversation with John and me on a variety of topics before heading off to play video games or draw. John and I love discussions in which she is vibrantly engaged, exploring a topic she is passionate about, engaging in wordplay, or just telling us a story. Most evenings, Beckett rushes off right after dinner, but interestingly, if we go out to eat, he's the one who entertains us with his thoughts, more so than his sister.

The first summer after I retired is one of my family favorites. On the weeks they didn't have camp, the kids and I explored various waterfalls in our area. On nice days, we would just pick one and go see it. On weekends, John would go with us to those that were further away. We got to be outside, enjoying nature, and sometimes play in the water features, spending time as a family. Our children discovered that there are hidden jewels all over the place if you just know where to look for them. They still call it our "waterfall summer."

Every once in a while, I will suggest to the family that I could get a part-time job so we could have a little more money for camps and vacations. Each and every time, my family tells me no; they would rather have me home. Since I would rather be home, it works out well for us all.

CHAPTER 12

NEW MANIFESTATIONS

When I'm discouraged I recall

My thoughts are all that's in my way

I can climb the highest wall

If I remember to say

What I'm trying to do is difficult, but I can do it

I just haven't done it yet

What I'm working on is challenging, but I'll get through it

I just haven't finished yet

—*"Power of Yet"*

MANY TIMES ALONG our journey I've said that it's like playing whack-a-mole. You think you've discovered what will work for one thing, but then it pops up in a different way or another thing rears its head. My observation is that when the stressors in April's life increase or she's beginning to make great strides in an area of competency, her autism manifests in new or different ways. As the schoolwork became more difficult and the demands and expectations for group work or social interactions became higher, we began to see new or increased changes in how her behaviors would compensate to cope.

Education

With all the class changes in junior high, April began to hate being late to class or showing up at the wrong location if it had been changed. Whenever either would happen, it would create a great deal of distress for her.

In seventh grade, April's paraprofessional (another wonderful person in April's life) had a health issue that required her to be out of work for a number of months. The school district was unable to have reliable substitute paraprofessionals on hand, and April was on her own for most of those months. I received an email from her math teacher informing me April was not doing her homework.

When I questioned April about it, she said the teacher put the homework assignment on the board at the end of class, and she didn't copy it down, because she was afraid of being late to her next class. Her paraprofessional normally took care of copying the assignment under those conditions. I relayed the information back to her teacher. He chose to start handing April a piece of paper with the assignment on it sometime during the class as he was walking by her desk.

As a parent and advocate for my child, I have found that when an issue arises in a general education classroom such as the one above, the best way to handle it is to inform the teacher what the specific problem is and suggest a few different solutions, but to let the teacher decide which works best for him/her in that classroom. I also try to stay out of the loop of school supports. By that, I mean I would not want a possible solution to be a teacher emailing me the assignments to give to April; that would increase her dependency on me for schoolwork.

For example, with April's need to fidget, some teachers preferred to sit her at the back of the class so she could fidget without disrupting her classmates; others preferred to sit her up front so they could keep her on task. I believe in affording teachers the respect that they can find a good option that works best in their classroom environment and that meets our daughter's needs once they know what the issue is. If I attempted to micromanage a classroom, I would not only alienate the educators but also deprive our daughter the experience of discovering that there is more than one solution to a problem.

∽

One of the issues I have experienced with some general education teachers at the higher grades is that they do not always communicate well with parents until there is a problem, as the teacher compares the behavior of the autistic child with the behavior of neurotypical developing teenagers. This creates additional concerns for special needs parents as our ability to determine whether there is a detrimental pattern of behavior developing in our child(ren) is significantly hindered by the lack of information.

I do understand and support the idea that teenagers need to take more responsibility for their schoolwork and suffer the consequences, but as a special needs parent, it is also important that I know that homework isn't being turned in or classwork is not being accomplished. If one teacher contacts me about a single assignment, I'm not going to do much about it unless I'm asked to step in, but if three to four teachers are saying similar things at the same time, I am going to get involved.

For example, in eighth grade, April began exhibiting the typical teenage I-can-get-it-done-before-class routine and then shutting down during class behaviors that didn't work so well with the higher complexity of the coursework combined with her autism. Unfortunately, no one thought to inform Hope or me until three weeks into it all. It took us months to get April back on track. It was the first time April faced a very real possibility of failing classes after being on the honor roll every previous year. The outcome was an increase of everyone's workload and expenditure of effort that could have been avoided had I had the information right away so I could recognize a pattern was developing.

On the other hand, other general education teachers are great at communicating. Knowing that Beckett was still developing in certain areas, Beckett's eighth grade Honors Language Arts teacher would reach out to me whenever there was a project he was having difficulty with during class time or if it was something that required inferring information from a text. Letting me know he needed extra support at home to be successful was just what he and I needed.

Wandering

Wandering is not unusual with autistic children and can be quite frightening for their parents. When the children were younger, we spent a lot of time outdoors in our large, fenced-in yard and never noticed any wandering tendencies on April's part. In junior high, though, we began to see her go onto the pool deck alone and just meander around the pool, occasionally stopping to pick up a leaf or stick. Despite our constant reminders that she has to tell us she is going outside, when the need hits, off she goes without a word. We continue the reminders in the hopes that she will eventually think to tell us, but she is now a teenager, so I do not have high hopes we'll be successful. Instead, I just moved my laptop to an area where I could see the back door and pool deck so I would know when she left the house.

Sensory & Dress

When Beckett and April were still toddlers and young enough to bathe together, we discovered that April liked the water much hotter than Beckett did. We would fill the bathtub halfway with the temperature set at a level comfortable for Beckett, put him in the bathtub furthest away from the faucet and let April turn up the temperature to her liking on her side of the bathtub for a while.

April still likes her showers extremely hot. John, Beckett, and I have all learned to turn the temperature control on one of our showers to the center before turning on the water, since each of us has been accidentally scalded after April has used that shower. However, for the past couple years, she has begun taking multiple hot showers per day, usually after you remind her to do something that she does not want to do or she believes will be difficult. It's as if she requires the increased sensory input to calm herself in advance.

✑

April also began wearing the same purple shirts most days for a couple years when school stressors increased. I began to get emails from teachers suggesting she had a hygiene problem, and I would have to explain that she had multiple T-shirts that were the same, so they were clean even if lacking in variety. I think the shirts were a way of taking one choice off her plate during a time when she was expected to start making more choices and having increased social interactions for her schoolwork. I also believe the shirts aided in calming her with their familiar feel and comfort.

Somewhere along the line, April started sleeping in her clothes instead of changing into pajamas, then putting on new clothes in the morning. In vain, I keep trying to get her back into the habit of pajamas because I think it will be another signal to her brain that it is time to sleep so she will have less instances of her hamster on the wheel keeping her awake at night.

Physical Contact

April's tolerance for physical contact has changed as she's aged. We began noticing that we were getting more sideways hugs and that she didn't want the nighttime cuddles before bedtime, so John and I began adjusting to her cues. She doesn't like to share a bed unless it is necessary (when we are on vacation), but still occasionally wants me close to her at night during extremely stressful times, like when there has been a death in the family. During those few needful nights, I would lie in bed near her, not touching her, and she would reach out to hold my hand while she slept. I'm not sure she realizes how much I treasure the moments when she reaches out to me for the physical comfort that works best for her.

Stereotypes

There are a number of stereotypes about autistic people that are inaccurate. One is that they cannot lie. That is untrue. It may be more difficult at times for them, but in April's case with the homework assignments, she was able to lie to me about the work being completed. Even as I began asking very specific questions to reduce the chances that she could find wiggle room in her responses, she still was able to tell untruths. She is aware that we find lying to us the worst behavior of all.

Another stereotype is that autistic people are unemotional, uncaring, unfeeling, or lacking in empathy. As many of their difficulties originate in the emotional, feeling part of their brains, I find this to be illogical. Regardless, our daughter is the same girl who once became so upset that we had to remove her from a christening ceremony for her cousin because she thought they were hurting the baby. She is the same child who recently wrote an essay about how she broke down crying at a club meeting about John's mother's death years prior and how close she had felt to her. Had you seen her and her grandmother together, you might not have thought that was the case, but April had a great deal of love for her grandmother and obviously was secure in her grandmother's love for her.

I believe what occurs in many autistic people is that they spend a great deal of time attempting to ignore or avoid their emotions because they unconsciously associate all emotions with the extreme fight-or-flight responses that they expend so much time and effort controlling. I have the impression sometimes that it's as if they are trying not to open their own perceived chaotic, emotional Pandora's box. Emotions are unpredictable, tricky things, and for many people, neurotypical or autistic, the more intense, difficult emotions can be scary and overwhelming.

The fact that it can take years before autistic children are able to successfully cope with sensory input means that they have, in effect, missed much of the time neurotypical children have been instinctually learning information processing, pragmatic language, and social awareness skills. Because so many of their coping strategies are spent trying to shut down the same area of their brain that processes facial expressions, it also creates a dichotomous situation for them.

All of this effectively puts autistic children behind the power curve in the neurotypical environment. They are now attempting to catch up in a world of unspoken, ever-changing social rules. And considering the fact that they have been bombarded with strong, overwhelming, primal emotions created by sensory overload fight-or-flight responses while young, it really isn't surprising to me that they may unconsciously begin to believe that all difficult emotions are to be avoided. It seems to me that it's just an offshoot of their survival mechanism.

We have been trying to teach April that emotions are neither good nor bad; they just are. It is what we do with those emotions that is important. We also remind her that avoiding the emotions only makes everything worse because you cannot make good decisions about what to do with those emotions if you ignore them. All of these teachings were also reinforced during her EASE therapy, which I will elaborate on later in the book.

Comfort Items

Starting in sixth grade, April began experimenting with wearing bandannas and different scarfs around her neck. She finally settled on two lighter-weight winter scarfs, then reduced it to one favorite. She wears that scarf every day, even to bed, and growls at me when I tell her I need to wash it. Hope, in an attempt to have April not wear it during the hotter months and to choose a more seasonally appropriate one, found herself without a counterargument when April's reply was "So you're telling me I can't eat ice cream in the winter, just because it's cold out?"

This year, I asked April to consider taking off her scarf and wearing it around her wrist just long enough for school pictures. Her question to me was "Are you telling me not to be myself?" My response: "No, I'm saying I have lots of pictures with you in the scarf, and I would like some without it." I did warn her, though, for senior pictures, I expect some without her scarf and some with it. That gives her three years to get used to the idea.

৵

Christmas 2017 saw the arrival of a new member of our household, a small Pokemon character plush toy named Torchic, who resembles an orange chicken. Torchic quickly became a new comfort item for

April and began to accompany her everywhere. Another larger stuffed Pokemon toy, Rowlet, who looks like a round owl, also showed up at the same time and starting going to school and spending the day in April's backpack in her locker. Both Rowlet and Torchic still sleep with her at night.

After it became apparent that Torchic was going to be a regular addition to April's classes, I began to receive emails concerned about April's maturity level. I haven't been worried about her needing Torchic to help her cope and relieve her stress. I find it interesting how the neurotypical world is sometimes a bit hypocritical when it comes to items like this.

I know of adults who still sleep with cherished childhood stuffed animals, have to have bobble-head toys on their work desks, go to Pokemon tournaments, attend various "Cons," play Dungeons and Dragons regularly, carry good-luck items, etc. I don't consider any of these items and activities any more or less mature, but it seems that they are acceptable to the neurotypical world because they are not always visible, considered a quirk, or because a number of people participate socially in the activity.

As a mother of an autistic teenager, my only issues with Torchic are whether or not he takes a bath regularly and the fact that he likes to state he loves April more than I do.

Chapter 13

Puberty

Life is change; it touches us all

Trust yourself; trust me

To catch you if you fall.

THERE WAS A day early on in fourth grade when April was home sick from school. Since it was just us girls, I thought it was a good time to start puberty discussions in earnest. As I explained the changes in her body that would start at some point, I could see the fear in her eyes. There are many types of transitions that can be scary for those with autism, but those over which they have no control, don't know what it will look or feel like, or when it will start or stop can feel overwhelming. To lighten the mood a little, I added, "Oh, and at some time during this process, you will suddenly think I am the stupidest person in the world. That's normal and lasts for a couple years. We may argue about it at times, but it will all happen the way it's supposed to." April's response: "Mom, if I ever tell you you're stupid, don't believe me. You're the smartest person I know." I wasn't the only one laying the groundwork for the future that day.

Since April already has some sensory issues, I bought a number of different brands of menstrual pads for her to try long before Mother Nature would decide they were needed. I patiently explained every step of what she needed to do when she started her period, including how to properly dispose of used pads, and had her repeat the steps back to me and show me. I had her wear one of each brand for a day to find out if there were any brands that might cause a sensory issue. The last thing I wanted was to find out there was a sensory problem for her with a feminine product during her first menstrual cycle. My efforts long before they were absolutely necessary enabled April to handle that part of puberty without incident and, most importantly, without additional stress. She and I both have an app that can track her cycle, but she often forgets to open the app to put the information in.

April's body developed early, and purchasing appropriate female undergarments that fit correctly became difficult. I finally had to take her for a proper bra fitting, concerned that the circumstances would cause a meltdown. She didn't feel capable of answering the saleswoman's questions, but handled the situation well otherwise. The saleswoman told April that a lot of girls her age cry and become very embarrassed, and she was impressed with April's composure. As I was checking out, I learned that the saleswoman had a younger son with ASD; perhaps April sensed the unspoken understanding during the fitting.

I taught April how to examine her breasts monthly once the bodily changes of puberty began. I had obtained some shower signs (similar to the Do Not Disturb signs you see hung on hotel room doors) that explained the process with pictures and hung them in a shower for her.

April is very cautious around knives and as such, and isn't comfortable with razors yet. So, I taught her how to properly use a hair removal product for the hair on her legs and underarms. I still have to remind her to use it.

For the past several years, April has been accompanying me to the gynecologist so that she can observe and become familiar with what happens during this uncomfortable but necessary annual exam. My doctor has been wonderful, offering to answer any questions April may have about anything that happens during the visit. A mother's love knows no boundaries.

෯

With puberty comes acne. It hasn't been easy trying to teach both children that they need to be washing their faces daily, as well as using astringent/toner and acne medicine when necessary. I've tried to make it as easy as possible for them by providing special wipes, for example, but even with prompts and reminders, I'm facing resistance. I am still in the process of determining whether there is a sensory issue or something else that is causing this particular task to be so undesirable to each of them.

As hormones change, so does body odor. As April takes so many showers, I am not certain how much deodorant she may be using; I suspect none at all. One evening, Beckett lifted his arms for whatever reason, and I got a strong whiff and told him deodorant was now a necessary item in his hygiene routine. In typical teenage-boy fashion, he lifted his arm again, stepped closer to me, and asked, "What? You don't like my man musk?" He recently discovered that is he now taller than me, and we've begun hearing his voice change intermittently.

Personal Facebook Post - August, 2019

I had an annual doctor's appointment today. Beckett questioned what it was for and April answered with a blunt, but fairly accurate response.

Beckett's quip? "I hope the doctor can be of cervix to you." Yep, our son definitely inherited his dad's sense of humor and made his dad proud. LOL! (Honestly, I thought John was going to cry from laughing so hard.)

John is the king of puns, and it seems our children have inherited his sense of humor. April is able to wield humorous sarcasm and irony fairly well too, taking more after me in that respect. Combining these traits with puberty, sassy teenagers are the norm in our household. I am quite happy to hear it, but do expend some effort ensuring that both of them understand when it is not appropriate.

I have often said to family and friends that April popped out of the womb already a teenager. Some of what we attributed to her being strong-willed may have also stemmed from her autism. In elementary school, she briefly developed an interest in curse words. We would repeatedly explain that her vocabulary was such that she could express herself quite well without swearing. But it became more of an obsession for her in junior high. She would go through periods where we needed to correct her often, then a lull, before repeating the cycle.

Now, John works in construction and I was an air traffic controller; neither one of us is a stranger to hearing or using curse words. But we have been very successful in not modeling that language in front of our children. The following is what I posted on my Facebook page after April unsuccessfully attempted to buy a $20 gift card for herself with cash I had given to her and her brother to pick up several needed items at the grocery store while I waited outside.

Personal Facebook Post - September 28, 2019

So, yesterday, I'm having a discussion with my daughter about how my money is not her money and even if she ends up choosing to live with us until she's 45 or I kick the bucket, she will, at some point, be getting a job, paying room & board and contributing toward food costs. I then added something to the effect of "If you think you'll be able to somehow avoid becoming a responsible adult and not having to work and pay your own way, you need to know now that that sh*t ain't happening."

She gives me a shocked look and says, "You almost never swear."

Me: "Oh, I'm an expert at swearing; I just choose not to do so around you kids."

With a hopeful, pleading look directed at me, she whispers, "Teach me ..."

LOL!

So many truly useful things I could teach her (like how to tell someone *exactly* where to go without curse words and have them thank you afterwards for the "advice") and *she* wants to learn how to drop epithets like a sailor.

(BTW, my answer was "Become a responsible adult and I'll be happy to give you a few pointers.")

In our household, there are certain things that are non-negotiable. Common courtesy— *excuse me, please,* and *thank you*—has been modeled, taught, and expected by us since Beckett and April's earliest years. Regular medical visits to maintain their health as well as taking any required medications are in the non-negotiable category. Beckett and April expect to receive some sort of discipline from us if they ever violate safety rules, whether physical or virtual. They have never gone into our pool without an adult present, although they are teenagers now, so we may have to revise that to a buddy rule.

One of those non-negotiables is that we do not intentionally hurt people, either verbally or physically. This is especially important during disagreements. John and I are fortunate that our children get along very well and rarely argue. Even some of the usual sibling it's-my-turn arguments are settled quickly if John or I tell them that we want them to work it out and if we end up having to do it, our solution will be to take the item away from both of them.

However, now that they are teenagers, a little more discord is evident as each child tries to establish where his/her own personal boundaries are. If you didn't know them well, you would probably think Beckett holds the title of dominant twin; the reality is that it's April.

The two of them are getting more experience fighting to be happy, rather than fighting to be right. John and I do a lot of coaching to help them express their feelings in a productive way, especially with Beckett still having difficulties with his anger regulation and April's tendency to think she is a bad person when she is stressed. Much like his father, Beckett is a peacemaker, many times giving in to keep said peace, but he's now feeling the need to stand up for himself more often. We remind them that after a disagreement, both of them should feel respected, heard, and understood, even if they don't get everything they want.

❧

Sometimes I believe that April's autism has been a very good thing for our mother-daughter relationship as we go through the puberty transition. April's core personality is much like mine: strong-willed, independent, intelligent, caring, and holding strong convictions with more than a little bit of attitude and humor thrown in. With her autism, I'm in the position of doing my best to help her find ways to reveal those qualities to the neurotypical world in a stress-free manner that works for her. Had she been neurotypical, she and I would probably have been at loggerheads, arguing for years already, each stubbornly holding her ground, and our household would've been filled with far more drama and teenage angst. I think, with her autism, the worst of our family drama and angst came much earlier.

❧

John and I often email each other links to articles or videos that we believe the other will find interesting, useful, funny, or worthy of discussion. Once the children were allowed email addresses, I began doing the same with them. Recently, John and I were discussing an article about masking in autism in front of the children, and April quietly said, "Masking is exhausting." Beckett didn't understand the term, so April explained it to him.

April's comment led to a long, frank discussion where John and I told her that we did not want nor expect her to pretend to be neurotypical; we just wanted her to continue growing into her best self. We said that everything we do as parents is to help her find the most effective ways for her to cope with her autism so she can function in the neurotypical environment with minimal stress and achieve what she wants in life—while remaining true to who she is. We informed her that we didn't want her autism to limit what she felt she could accomplish any more than we would have had she had been born without a hand or foot. John and I acknowledged that her challenges are more difficult in some ways since her autism is invisible to others—until it isn't—but we hoped that she knew that she didn't need to hide her autism from the world. We also explained that if we had felt she should mask her autism, we would have made different choices for her along the way. Whether or not April internalized what we discussed or took it to heart remains to be seen.

⌁

Knowing the chances are increased that April may at some point struggle with her sexual preferences and/or identity, John and I have explained to April that during puberty, hormones are in flux and can cause confusion. We have told her that we love her no matter what, but there is no hurry or need to decide on the "correct" label at this point in her life. We have also reassured her that it would be her body, not her mind, that determines her sexual preferences and gender identity and that it would come with more interpersonal experiences.

John and I only care that April is true to herself and someday finds a relationship with someone who loves her as she is and that she loves that person in return. Our biggest concern is that her autism might guide her choices by intellectually selecting what she believes *should* be. All we can do is remain supportive and hope that she eventually recognizes her actual needs, whatever they may be.

Self-Injurious Behaviors

Several weeks after finishing my first draft of this book, I received a call from the school that April had exhibited self-injurious behaviors (SIBs) the week prior: pulling her hair, smacking her head with her palm, bending her fingers backwards, and poking her hand with a pencil. Unfortunately, no one, including April, was able to tell me what had precipitated the incident. We had only observed two instances of her smacking her head with her palm before this; once in elementary school and once in junior high school. Both times, the behaviors ceased when we told her that it was an unacceptable way to cope with her stress.

I have since seen April exhibit SIBs twice at home, both for the same situation on Christmas Day. After opening gifts, she smacked her head with her palm, cried, and called herself stupid. We immediately told her to stop and breathe. She ceased, but was still unable to explain. We understood only that she didn't receive something she had really wanted but that she had felt unable to communicate to us. She felt it was too complicated to explain to us.

During our bedtime ritual, she became frustrated and upset again attempting to explain and started to bend her fingers backwards. I again told her to stop and breathe. I reminded her that she was not allowed to hurt herself under any circumstances. Once she was calm, I was able to ascertain what the gift was—it involved a video game that was only available through digital code from outside the United States—and that she would be able to obtain it with a gift card, which we bought the following day.

The new manifestation of SIBs obviously concerns us, and we'll be tracking any future instances closely. However, I also see it as an indicator that she is making progress in other areas. Historically, when April starts making large strides in an area of competency, her autism begins to compensate in previously unseen ways as she seeks to balance the increased stressors. When viewed through the lens of her recent growth (to be covered in a later chapter, Self-Advocacy) her extreme frustration at not being able to find a way to explain herself on Christmas Day makes sense. She knows how it feels to succeed at asking for what she wants or needs but is not yet reliably able to do so. She still needs more practice.

We need to guide her in a fashion that does not allow the SIBs to become a part of her new normal. Fortunately, April responds to the verbal prompt "No, you are not allowed to hurt yourself. Breathe." We have discussed various options if she feels the need to do something with her hands: gripping a desk or table edge, a book, a squeeze toy, or even Torchic. All we can do is continue to help her learn how to keep herself safe and self-regulate when she feels similar urges.

CHAPTER 14

IDEA VS. ADA/504

The unseen future beckons you
I feel your apprehension and fear
Stay strong; don't be blue.
You've got this, my dear.

THE INDIVIDUALS WITH Disabilities Education Act (IDEA) and the American with Disabilities Act (ADA) were both signed into law in the United States in 1990. In 2008, the ADA law was amended and included a clarification of the definition of disability found in Section 504 of the Rehabilitation Act enacted in 1973. These are important in the life of an autistic person, as IDEA pertains to his/her public-school education, while ADA applies to both school and postsecondary-school life, whether that is further schooling or employment.

IDEA provides federal financial assistance to state and local education agencies to guarantee special education and related services to children in the public-school system, ages three to twenty-one, who are in K-12 education and determined by a multidisciplinary team to be eligible, within one or more of thirteen specific disability categories—one of which is autism. According to the law's language, special education means "specially designed instruction at no cost to the parents, to meet the unique needs of the child with a disability."

ADA is a civil rights law prohibiting discrimination solely on the basis of disability in employment, public services, and accommodations. This covers any individual with a disability who (1) has a physical or mental impairment that substantially limits one or more life activities, (2) has a record of such impairment, or (3) is regarded as having such an impairment. Further, the person must be qualified for the program, service, or job. Reasonable accommodations are required for eligible individuals with a disability to perform essential functions of the job. This applies to any part of the special education program that may be community-based and involve job training and placement. ADA protections apply to public schools and nonsectarian private schools, but not religious schools.

It is salient that if your child has an IEP, he/she has the protections afforded by both IDEA and ADA, but if your child has a 504 plan, he/she is only afforded the protections under ADA, as Section 504 is defined by ADA, not IDEA. The reason for this is that not all children with a disability or impairment automatically qualify for special education services. ADA provides for accommodations to receive the same free appropriate public education (FAPE) provided to non-disabled students (e.g., wheelchair access, Braille class materials, testing accommodations), while IDEA law provides for the full educational opportunity to all children with disabilities (e.g., course modifications). There are more procedures, protections, and safeguards in place for families under IDEA than ADA.

As April had been identified in pre-K as requiring early intervention services, it was an automatic process for our school district to do the testing necessary to qualify her for an IEP under IDEA. This means I have no practical experience with 504 plans.

Several years ago, a friend's child was diagnosed with autism partway through elementary school, and the district recommended a 504 plan. My friend contacted me for advice. After some quick research, I suggested that she begin with a 504 plan so her child could begin receiving some services immediately (no meeting necessary) and insist upon the district continuing with their evaluation to qualify her child for an IEP. As their family's journey living with the knowledge of autism was just beginning and they did not yet know what that would mean for their child, I wanted to ensure that they had access to as many services as may be needed to aid their child, now and in the future.

⋖⋗

There is an organization that works with our state Department of Education and Bureau of Special Education to provide professional development to aid stakeholders in improving special needs student outcomes in Pennsylvania. While the training is primarily geared towards educators, there are courses available to parents.

Early in eighth grade, Hope forwarded me an email for an upcoming day seminar on IEP planning for college and career transitions for students with autism. I was the only parent present that was not also in an education-related career. This was where I became aware that we should be preparing April to lead her own IEP meetings before she leaves the public-school system and making self-advocacy and executive function skills a higher priority at this stage.

In another seminar on the same subject this year, I learned that, according to the 2015 *National Autism Indicators Report: Transition into Young Adulthood*, 36 percent of young adults with autism attended any type of postsecondary education in their early twenties. Examples of postsecondary education include two-year or four-year colleges and vocational education. What surprised me was the fact that only 35 percent of those students graduated from that postsecondary education within eight years of high school graduation.[3] That means only about a third of the autistic students who do pursue postsecondary education actually complete it. Overall graduation rates within six years of high school for US two-year or four-year colleges and universities is about double that for all students, regardless of ability.[4]

3 National Longitudinal Transition Study-2, 2011.
4 National Center for Education Statistics.

The differences in IDEA and ADA mean that April will have to self-identify her autism if she requires accommodations in college and then coordinate with the professors herself. She will have to provide documentation of her diagnosis when she is requesting aid from a higher institution's disability services office, and a school district's IEP will not meet this requirement. Depending on the college, there may also be time or testing requirements for the diagnosis. Some of the supports she has in place now will not be available to her after high school, so another focus of ours is reducing those supports to only those that can be reasonably provided as accommodations in college or a workplace. Other supports may be available, but at an additional cost to her.

I am glad that April will have ADA protections in her postsecondary life, but realize that a greater deal of maturity and level of skills are expected of her at that earliest stage of her adult life than of neurotypical students for her to receive those protections. Those skills are amongst the most difficult for someone with autism: self-identification and asking for help, communication of her needs to each individual professor, and executive function skills to ensure everything necessary happens in a timely fashion, all within an unfamiliar environment during a transition. Our daughter has to be ready to take the lead on her own advocacy, while I'll have to shift to a background supportive role. Legally, I will no longer be able to speak for her even when she cannot or will not speak for herself.

To me, it feels like a double whammy that the areas that are most difficult for autistic people are the ones in which they absolutely have to have developed sufficient competency to obtain the protections afforded to them under law; especially since the science behind their neurological disability supports the fact that their particular disability adversely affects those areas. However, they are also adults at that stage and have, and should have, the rights afforded to them by their adult status. I'm not sure that there is a good compromise to be had within the legal system that best meets all their needs.

❧

CHAPTER 15

TRANSITIONING TO HIGH SCHOOL

Each step takes you further from me
But it is all as it should be.

I HAVEN'T MENTIONED it before, but, historically, back-to-school shopping has not been a pleasant activity for any of us. Shopping for school supplies was easy; the children were happy to find new items and make their choices. Clothes were a different matter. Beckett dislikes wearing jeans; only shorts and sweatpants for him. Graphic and plain colorful T-shirts are popular with him, so it isn't as difficult for him to make choices. But April has more sensory issues, so material softness and texture is a factor. There have been years when she decided on pullovers in one or two plain colors and won't wear anything else. Occasionally, she will pick a T-shirt that supports autism, but has mostly gravitated away from graphic tees. However, it is usually difficult for her to choose an item—yes or no —and I would spend time, sometimes painfully long times, trying to ascertain what she would actually wear. With puberty, she now has a womanly form and does not like to wear anything too low cut. In the past, for shirts that she liked but showed too much cleavage, I would sew the neckline closed to a height that she liked.

For our clothes shopping for high school, I changed my modus operandi. We didn't go to our usual haunts but to a store that catered more to the teen/young adult crowd. I would feel an item, and if I didn't think it would be a sensory problem for April, I would hold it up and say, "Would you like to try this on?" If she didn't immediately answer with a yes or maybe, I would put it back and move on without comment. I chose a variety of colors to see what her preferences might be this year. I was pleased to see her pick different colors to try.

There was one button-down shirt that was well outside her normal style of dress. It was harvest gold with large blue and white flowers. I held it up and asked her if she thought it was something she might like. When she said she didn't know, I just put it back. Later, we saw the same shirt on a mannequin, and I pointed it out to her. She tried on the other clothes, liking all of them, but a couple of the jersey-knit tops were too low cut. I expressed my concern that if I tacked the necklines, it would ruin the look of the shirts. April said, "I can just wear tank tops underneath. It's the style anyway." She had come up with an acceptable, workable solution on her own, and I added tank tops to the list of things to buy.

April finished in the fitting room before Beckett did and while I was waiting for him, she went off and came back with the harvest gold shirt and asked if she could try it on. Of course I said yes. It is now her favorite shirt. This year's shopping was the most enjoyable shopping trip we've ever had, partly due to her growing maturity, partly because I decided to reduce both our stress loads by not even trying to make her choose whether or not she liked something if it didn't immediately appeal to her. Lesson learned, Mom.

∽

I believe I found the transition to high school far more worrisome than either of our children did. While I was friendly with some of the staff, including the principal, there was no PTA there. Unless our children decided on activities with large booster clubs, it was unlikely I would be spending much time in the school during school hours. Beckett decided to drop his band activities because he wasn't sure how difficult the schoolwork would be, and he wanted to be sure he had a study hall period.

I read *Helping Students with Autism Spectrum Disorder Express their Thoughts and Knowledge in Writing: Tips and Exercises for Developing Writing Skills* and decided that the most useful-sounding supports suggested that fit April's needs would go into her IEP before the transition. I hope that these supports will better prepare her for college work and perhaps beyond; they are supports that can be reasonably accommodated in a postsecondary educational environment.

Armed with the information I learned during the seminars about increasing successful postsecondary outcomes, I sat down with April to review her IEP, support by support. We were able to reduce and, in many instances, eliminate some supports that had been in her IEP for years. I informed Hope, and she made the changes to April's transitional IEP meeting document.

I explained to April that one of our goals was that she would be taking the lead on her IEP meetings before the end of high school. I let her know that we would be taking smaller steps to start and adding more each year.

One of those steps was having her prepare an About Me page for her transitional IEP meeting. I informed her that she should include her likes and dislikes, what creates stress for her, what helps her when she's stressed, special interests, and any other information *she* felt was important for her teachers to know about her and her autism. I told her she did not have to write an essay, unless she wanted to, but could do a bulleted or numbered list. I also suggested that she could do a PowerPoint presentation or anything else she wanted that would share the pertinent information. While I had to do a lot of prompting to have her complete it, she eventually finished her list and I made copies for the meeting.

April received a lot of positive feedback for her contribution to the meeting. Her future (now current) support teacher, Sam, suggested that she keep refining her list and give copies to all her teachers at the high school. April and I discovered that the principal had a son on the spectrum who would be starting college in the fall. He was very supportive of suggestions, made by April's junior high teachers, that some of the students April had been socializing with during lunch and successfully doing group work with be assigned the same lunch period or classes whenever appropriate and possible.

We discussed which classes should be honors classes, specifically civics. Based on his knowledge of the course and teachers available, Sam suggested that April might be a better fit in the honors course. April had already shown interest in historical displays on subjects like women's suffrage, black civil rights, LGBTQ rights, union activism, etc., when we visited museums, so I thought the honors course was appropriate for those reasons as well. April did not feel comfortable making the decision and asked me to make it for her.

John's unexpected illness earlier in the year and subsequent time out of work meant we did not have the disposable income to send the children to any camps during the summer before high school like we normally would. They spent the summer staying up late, sleeping in, drawing, playing in the pool, and doing whatever teenagers do on their computers, phones, and video games. It was unintentional on our part, but I think the laziness of that summer contributed to an easier transition to high school for April.

With the upcoming transition to high school and April smack-dab in the middle of puberty and all that entails, I started researching the possibility of having her see a therapist for extra support throughout the transition. I was having difficulties finding one who had experience with autistic teen girls and would also accept our health insurance.

Serendipitously, in the midst of my search, Hope forwarded me an email about a research study at the Center for Excellence in Autism Research at the University of Pittsburgh to evaluate a new treatment therapy for emotional regulation. The new therapy, Emotional Aware-ness and Skills Enhancement (EASE), is a mindfulness therapy and study participants would either receive traditional cognitive therapy or EASE for 16 weeks. I'll discuss the therapy more in the following chapter, Self-Advocacy.

∽

A couple weeks before school started, I received a phone call from the high school principal asking if our children would like another tour of the school to ease the transition. He personally took us around the school, explaining differences in procedures from the junior high, such as having the same homeroom teacher and guidance counselor for all four years, how to request library time for a study hall, etc. The high school also started a Link Crew transition program where incoming freshmen received an upperclassman mentor, and Beckett and April attended that initial welcome before the beginning of the school year.

Both the children joined the Gay-Straight Alliance Club, which happens to be led by teacher advisors they already knew. April, espe-cially, looks forward to the social interaction of the club and there has already been a party and a roller-skating rink event, which both children enjoyed. I have been unsuccessful discovering why Beckett hasn't wanted to join the PA Club, which is responsible for the school's morning video announcements. I worry that it is fear, not a lack of interest.

∽

As I mentioned earlier, Beckett is on the mathematics fast-track. I noticed that his grade was falling in his Honors Algebra II class, with his tests and quizzes bringing his grade down significantly. Any time I questioned him about what he believed the problem was, he would get frustrated and tell me he didn't have enough time to complete the work. Believing he did not understand the concepts well enough, I had him start working on Khan Academy. I was contacted by Beckett's teacher at the end of the first quarter to discuss his lack of progress.

His teacher assured me that Beckett was giving the class his best efforts, taking notes, participating, and turning in homework. She believed he may need another year for his brain to grow and suggested that I talk to him about transferring to another class. John and I sat Beckett down and reassured him that we were not upset with him since he had been giving the class his best efforts and wasn't being lazy. We told him that it was okay not to understand, but we wished he had told us earlier so we could help him. We also let him know that we wanted him to be pushed to learn more, but not to feel frustrated every day and like he couldn't catch up.

We transferred him to the Academic Algebra II class, where the material is taught at a slower pace. His grade has climbed back up, and he is feeling happy and confident again. But now we know that he does have difficulties asking for help.

✍

We were less than halfway through Beckett and April's freshman year, and I, much more than either of them, was experiencing some growing pains in the adjustment. Sam, April's support teacher, hadn't been as responsive to my emails as Sunny and Hope had been. I wasn't yet sure that it was because that's how he is or because he was also the head football coach and was busy with football season. I had never met April's paraprofessional, who had no previous experience with April's personality and needs. There had been a couple instances where the paraprofessional had attempted to aid April, but in ways that were more detrimental than helpful to April's progress. I understood that everyone was still learning about one another and that missteps would occur. I had been trying to find a balance that worked for all of us, but I was beginning to feel that it was time for me to arrange a meeting to clarify what my expectations were.

CHAPTER 16

SELF-ADVOCACY

Insecurity, fear of the unknown;
You say you can't, but that's not true.
Speak for yourself; you deserve the best.
They don't know what you need, but you do.
Confidence comes when you ask for what will help
To make your dreams come true.

THE FIRST TIME April advocated for herself, unprompted, for what she needed, it was in anger, partway through junior high. We had attended a long family affair the day before. The conversation went something like this:

Me: April, you'll have to stop playing video games and go get all the dirty clothes and sort them in the laundry room.

April: (no response)

Me: April, honey, did you hear me? You need to get the dirty clothes so I can wash them.

April: (angry) Well, excuuuusssse me if I need extra time to de-stress after the party yesterday!

Me: (surprised) Whoa! This is the first I've ever heard that you needed time to de-stress after an event. If you need more time, of course you'll have it. But you will still have to get the dirty clothes once you've finished. I'm more than happy to accommodate your autism, but your autism doesn't give you an excuse not to do your part.

After all was said and done, I told April that while I wasn't happy with her tone, I was extremely proud that she had let me know what she needed in order to cope with one aspect of her autism. This was the only instance of self-advocacy on April's part before she would be guided in therapy to do so during her transition into high school.

April was accepted into the EASE 16-week study. We were able to time it so that she would be about halfway through it when she started high school. Fortunately for us, she was placed in the mindfulness therapy group; it has made a significant difference in all our lives. While I needed some distance from earlier years to identify areas in which April had experienced the most growth, I can say with a great deal of confidence that when I reflect back on her high school years in a decade's time, we'll see that these have been the years she has shown the greatest growth in advocating for herself.[5]

With the exception of April identifying her levels of distress and naming what she experiences at each level (a barometer, if you will), the EASE study didn't introduce any tools or insight that John and I had not already tried to give April on our own. The difference, I think, was April's maturity level, the voluntary participation in setting goals that were important to her, the structure of the therapy, the community sessions, and someone other than her parents guiding her and giving her the information.

5 As of this writing, the EASE study is still ongoing and overall results have not yet been published.

There were added benefits for me as well. Since we now have a barometer that we both understand, I can ask her where she is on her scale of distress and have a better idea of what she truly needs at that moment in time. Also, because I am concentrating on helping April with specific words that prompt her to use her training to calm her emotions, it enables me to focus better and longer on April's emotional regulation and not to rush ahead into finding solutions to the problem.

April was required to come up with her own plan to continue using what she had learned in the EASE program. During the therapy, April came up with her own prompts that she wanted people to use to remind her of her mindfulness training. After getting April's approval on the wording, I communicated those prompts to all her teachers in my annual new-school-year email. She also created her own designs for cards for her to use to remind herself that she was still learning. I printed her designs, made the cards and also made cards for the school's support staff to use for the mindfulness prompts. I even laminated them all for everybody.

Research has shown that if an individual does a short meditation each day, it will actually reduce the amount of stress he/she will feel in a future situation. I told April it was like building up a reserve of calm she could draw from when needed, and she added it to her plan. I offered an incentive to help keep her to it: if she performed her daily meditations at least 5 days a week and had a 5-minute conversation with someone she doesn't normally speak to once a month, then I would get her a $10 gift card each month. So far, it does not seem to be enough of an incentive for her to do her daily mediations. We're still working on that.

One night at dinner, we were talking about what day we would be going back-to-school shopping. Earlier in the year, I had purchased April a couple pairs of jeans online. (Keep in mind that this, and all the subsequent examples, occurred during April's EASE therapy or not long afterwards, all in a matter of a couple months.)

April: I need pants with front pockets.

Me: Okay. (pause) You know you're allowed to have opinions on your clothes, right?

April: The last jeans you bought didn't have front pockets. I usually keep Torchic in a front pocket, because when I put him in a back pocket, it hurts to sit down. I'm afraid of losing him.

Me: I didn't realize that you needed front pockets. Now that I know why it's important to you, I won't forget to make sure your pants have them.

The remainder of that conversation consisted of John and I telling her how thrilled we were that she spoke up for what she needed to cope. We also added that most people are more than happy to help her, but she has to let them know what she needs because they don't know; only she does. I told her it had never occurred to me to look for front pockets, and while it required very little effort on my part to help her meet that need, it made me feel good that I could do something that makes things easier for her.

Since I had paid good money for the online jeans without front pockets, I also asked her how she felt about coming up with a solution that might work for her to still wear those pants occasionally or when she wanted to dress up. We ended up deciding that a pocketbook with an outside pocket large enough for Torchic might work. He could still be close and she could touch him as needed without unzipping the pocketbook. We found one she liked that met the requirements, added some feminine basics to the zipped portion and the pocketbook now resides in her backpack in her locker for whenever it may be needed as a backup plan.

❧

I can always tell when April has something to say that she feels is important but is uncomfortable communicating. It has to do with how she makes or doesn't make eye contact. Another dinnertime conversation she unconsciously started with her tell:

April: (standing up) I have something to say that you might not like and I don't want you to get upset.

John: Okay.

Me: What is it you need to say?

April: I know you guys are huggers and that's how you like to show your affection. I'm not saying this to hurt you, but I don't like to hug as much as you two and it makes me uncomfortable to have people in my personal space.

John: You're right; Mom and I do like to hug to show our affection. I'm glad you told us how you feel.

Me: I'm so proud of you for advocating for yourself. (pause) You do know we are aware that you aren't as comfortable with hugs as your Dad and I, or even Beckett, right? We have tried to limit our hugs so you aren't uncomfortable, but if we're still doing it too much, we'll try to do even better.

April: (relieved) I know you love me. It's just that sometimes it feels you're in my personal space too much and it stresses me out.

John: I can't promise to never hug you again, so please don't ask me to do that.

April: Dad, just less hugs, not no hugs.

John: Okay. Can I give you a short hug now to show you how proud I am of you?

April: (mildly exasperated) Yes.

Before this conversation, we had already changed to high fives instead of hugs for some situations, and at night, if I had the impression she didn't want a hug or kiss, I had gotten in the habit of kissing my forefinger and momentarily touching it lightly to the tip of her nose as a substitute. I really am proud of her for telling us that we needed to continue to adjust our ways so that she isn't uncomfortable. Since this conversation, John has taken to just asking her beforehand and accepting whatever answer she gives without comment, judgment, or complaint. I sometimes do that too, but April and I have also started air-hugging or air-kissing, complete with a loud and cheerful "Air hugs!" or "Air kiss!" We have naturally fallen into this semi-flamboyant practice. It gives me the ability to express how often I would hug her if I could while letting her know I love and respect her enough to keep it virtual, and it leaves it up to April to decide if she wants more. If she does, she'll step closer to get a physical hug or kiss. The compromise suits both our personalities.

⌁

April has had difficulties verbally asking for help ever since elementary school, which was one of the reasons for her Break and Help cards. One day, she came home after school and…

April: (excitedly) Mom, I did a thing today.

Me: You did a thing!?! What thing did you do?

April: I didn't understand something in science and I told the teacher I didn't understand.

Me: So you asked for help? What happened?

April: He helped me.

Me: Do you understand now?

April: Yes.

Me: Wow! You told someone you needed help and you got what you needed. That's wonderful!

If you don't know someone with autism who has this particular issue, you may not understand how gigantic a step this was for April; she has been struggling with it (and all the accompanying anxiety) for over a decade. The pride and excitement she exhibited in wanting to tell me about the "thing" she had accomplished also let me know that April understood it was a very big breakthrough for her.

≪

Another day after school:

> **April:** I did two things today.
>
> **Me:** Two things!?! What were they?
>
> **April:** I asked for help in math class and my teacher helped me.
>
> **Me:** That's great! I'm glad you're getting what you need by speaking up for yourself. What was the other thing?
>
> **April:** I raised my hand to answer a question in science and I got it wrong.
>
> **Me:** (confused) Okay, you got the answer wrong. What happened then?
>
> **April:** Mom, you don't get it. I got the answer wrong and I didn't think to myself, "I'm so stupid." I didn't get upset for not having the right answer.
>
> **Me:** (light dawning) Baby girl, that's fantastic! I'm so proud of you.

One of the manifestations of April's autism has been an overwhelming need to be perfect in her schoolwork. The fear of being publicly wrong has held her back from participating more in her classes, and the hamster on the wheel with the negative self-talk would start spinning if she answered a question incorrectly in front of her peers. When she relayed this to me, she was excited about the fact that there was no negative self-talk or anxiety, and we were overjoyed to see her confidence growing as her emotional regulation improves.

≪

A few weeks ago, April came home and told me that her paraprofessional had said that Torchic and her sketchbook could no longer come out during class time. I told April that if she felt she needed or wanted either of her stress relievers, she was to use them, and I would see if I could find out what was going on. I sent an email to her support teacher asking where these changes had originated and why April or I hadn't been included in a decision to remove two stress relievers at once—which I, in no way, could support.

The next day I asked April if she had needed Torchic or her sketchbook. April's response: "Not so much today, but I made sure to take them out and put them on the corner of my desk in every class anyway just to spite her [paraprofessional]." I am proud of her standing up for what she needs, even if it is silently. And it shows me that if she feels it's important, her executive function skills will rise to the occasion. I had yet to hear back from her support teacher; hence the meeting I alluded to in an earlier chapter.

I have since met with Sam to talk about what he and other teachers may be noticing about April's school behaviors and discussed joint priorities for April's growth. He informed me that he had instructed April's paraprofessional to give April more space and distance, as she is capable of handling many situations without aid now. But Sam had noted that April has been exhibiting stress behaviors whenever there was a large, unstructured assignment in class. Sam has arranged with April's teachers to be informed beforehand of such assignments so that they can be broken down into smaller chunks. With his foreknowledge, April's paraprofessional will move in closer to April during these assignments so that our daughter is aware that there is support without her having to ask or look for it. Much like the bus situation in elementary school (i.e., knowing the rules were at hand in case she should forget them), I believe April can do it on her own, but to keep her anxiety levels low, she needs reassurance that there is a backup plan just in case.

Sam also had an idea on how to enable April to communicate with her paraprofessional when she finds it difficult to speak or is unwilling to speak in front of her peers: a journal specifically for that purpose, where she can write or draw what it is that's difficult for her. It has the benefits of allowing her the stress-relief of drawing and freeing her from the pressure to speak if she is uncomfortable. I like the creative solution; I hope April does too, and that it will be a good support for her.

I also took the opportunity to clarify my communication expectations with Sam. I explained that I had spent many years in air traffic control, am raising teenagers, one with autism, and in my world, *not acknowledged* equates to *not received*. He apologized and committed to doing better. Despite the misstep in our communication, I believe Sam and I will work well together, and if there are any future instances where I am not completely satisfied with response times to my emails, we will be able to find a solution together.

The following is something I posted on my Facebook page after April's last community session in the EASE study. At the time, April wasn't sure she wanted people to know it was therapy, but was fine with me using the word *training* instead.

Personal Facebook Post - October, 2019

I have to say how enormously PROUD I am of our daughter today. She's 14 weeks into a 16-week mindfulness training program designed specifically for teens/young adults living with autism. Part of the program is setting and meeting incremental personal goals based on what the trainee feels creates the most difficulty with their own emotional regulation.

Early on, April made it clear that outside of school stressors, she had the most difficulty with talking/socializing with new people and discussing anything to do with her own future plans after high school. So we set her end goal for the program as having a 5-10 minute conversation with a stranger and a separate family goal that she and I would have a longer conversation about future possibilities a couple months after her training was completed.

All along, I've been pointing out specific examples of how she's dealing with her anxiety much better, with fewer meltdowns overall *and her recovery time is *significantly* faster after the few incidents that she's experienced during this process.*

Well, this afternoon she met with a Pitt [University of Pittsburgh] recruiter (addressing both major stressors at the same time). Her instructor told me April had started out soft-spoken and anxious but pulled herself out of it. About halfway through the conversation, April—in a normal voice—very clearly stated, "I have autism. What kind of support services do you have available for someone like me?"

Baby girl hit the trifecta with that question by advocating for herself!!! From what I hear, April walked out of the recruiter's office elated, saying how confident she felt. John and I have always known that confident young lady was in there; I think (hope!) she's beginning to really internalize *she* has the power to feel that way more often than not. I can't even begin to express how much I want that for her.

Ecstatic, proud mama here trying not to cry...

As I write this, April's last session in the EASE study was over a month ago. In over six weeks, she has only had one significant meltdown at school where she had to take a break or couldn't speak. At home, she has also had one significant meltdown and several smaller ones in the same time frame. Before, April would need one to two hours to calm down after a significant meltdown at home; we're now down to five to ten minutes.

Recently, April has been on a special needs field trip to a local business and, on her own, decided to approach an employee at lunch, sit with him, and have a conversation. She also had a conversation at the roller-skating rink with their "skate ambassador."

In my recent conversation with Sam, it sounded like April has been experiencing some smaller moments of anxiety that she hasn't told me about. When I explained what had happened during my meeting with her support teacher, I asked her why she hadn't mentioned them. It took a few minutes before I could convince her to answer the question, but in the end it was because she didn't want me to worry about her.

I was touched by her concern for my feelings but let her know that I would worry about her even if she didn't have autism; it comes with the mom title. I explained that I couldn't do my best to help her find solutions that reduce her stress if she didn't communicate that stress to me. We'll see how it goes with April in the future, but it is another example of why timely communication between school and home is important.

I don't know whether April would have had the same results had she been able to participate in a similar mindfulness program when she was younger or if she needed a certain degree of maturity and competencies before the therapy could be truly effective. Maybe she just needed to feel ready to do it for herself. What I do know is that at this time in her life, the program was exactly what she needed. I have no doubt that once her confidence in her ability to regulate her emotions and handle unexpected situations becomes the new true resting point of *her* normal, our daughter will be unstoppable.

Personal Facebook Post - 2018

Baby girl just gave me the biggest-bestest-ever compliment and didn't even realize it. One of her birthday gifts from us was a T-shirt that says "Girls Can Do Anything." She looks at me and matter-of-factly says, "Well, of course they can. You've already proven that, Mom."

Baby girl, you're proving it now!

CHAPTER 17

THE FUTURE

Call on us when you need more;
Face to face, email, text, phone.
Our hands will lift; we'll help you soar
You don't ever have to go it alone.

APRIL IS WORRIED about getting a driver's license. She's afraid she might get distracted and hurt other people or herself. If she isn't able to obtain a driver's license, this could limit her options for postsecondary education and employment.

John and I would like both children to begin volunteering soon. I think April might enjoy helping at the local humane society, as she loves animals. Volunteering at a retirement or nursing home might be a better fit for Beckett. At some point, I expect part-time jobs to be on the list. Both volunteering and part-time employment would be good experiences and help develop executive function skills.

As of now, April would like to do something with art and is thinking graphic arts and design might be a possible career. I think that the animation field might be a good fit for her too, although I see her bringing designs to life for mechanical animations rather than working on storyboards. She took a career compatibility quiz for a school assignment and translation/languages also came up as a possible field that she might enjoy.

Regardless of what she chooses, college of some sort is most likely in her future, which means we have to look at all the potential issues with the transition beyond self-advocacy and executive function skills. Should she start in a summer session when there are fewer people around to acclimate to the campus with less stress? Would a college close to home be best, at least initially, so she's only dealing with the transition of high school to college and not of having to live on her own at the same time? Would part-time student status be more appropriate than full-time status for her first year or longer?

These types of questions have been on my mind for the past several years. Many of these decisions will have to be made closer to the time of the transition since we do not know yet how much and what type of progress she will have made by then. John and I have already talked about how community college at home for the first couple years would financially be best, and then Beckett and April could transfer to more expensive institutions to finish degrees in whatever fields they've chosen.

At the parent orientation for the high school, two other potential scenarios presented themselves. The first: Our school district has dual enrollment programs with a number of colleges close to home. The children could attend a couple classes together while still in high school, so April would have her brother for support in her college classes as she navigates the initial smaller transition. I might have to argue for it, but I would still be able to advocate for April as needed as she would not yet be an adult. Both would have some college credits to transfer as well, all at a reduced cost to our family. The second: Our school district has an alliance with a local career technical center, and one of the options offered is a two-year Commercial Art & Design program. While not a college per se, it might be a stepping stone, and they do have an agreement with our local community college that would transfer almost a full year of college credits upon successful completion. If this is something April is interested in, she could leave high school with a marketable skill, a head start on a college degree, and a better idea of which direction might suit her best. The downside is that Beckett would probably not attend with her, based on his interests and the course curriculum.

I have a meeting scheduled with their guidance counselor to discuss what is entailed for each option. John and I don't want to create additional stress for either child if the combined course load required for dual enrollment or the career technical center would be too great.

We also worry that Beckett, consciously or unconsciously, may only consider options that keep him close to April, instead of what may be best for *his* dreams. John and I would like to have him close to home initially, not only for financial reasons, but to ensure that his transition into postsecondary education goes smoothly as well. We realize that if he still wants to pursue professional animation/cartooning when he is older, he may have to go further afield to complete a degree or find work.

In the meantime, we'll need to do more research to determine which disability services are available at the institutions April may want to attend in the future. If her executive function skills are not as well developed as we hope by then, we may have to consider a gap year or a college that has specific aid available to help continue her development in that area at an additional cost. She will have decisions to make, and decisions for her, especially about the future, are not so easy right now. All we can do is have as much information as possible available and let her guide us towards what will be best for her.

Chapter 18

What I've Learned

When you forget to be afraid
Your inner light shines bright.
Working together, fear unmade
Opens the world to your light...

IN THE PREVIOUS chapters, I have attempted to provide you with the whys of our decisions as parents. Your decisions may not be the same since your whys may be different than ours. What we currently use and have used as supports for our children may not be the best choices for your autistic loved one. I believe if you base your decisions on your love for and knowledge of the complete child—not just the autistic part and his/her needs to grow (not your needs), you will be doing your best.

There are some things I have learned on our journey of living with autism that I believe will be helpful to parents and educators alike in guiding and supporting a child with autism. Hopefully, you will find some value in my shared experiences that will aid you on your journey.

Educate Yourself

Continuously. Learn as much as you can about autism, potential therapies, child development, education, psychology, and neurology as it pertains to your situation. Learn from as many different sources as you can. Learn what may fit your unique circumstances and your own (or autistic family's if you are an educator) belief system. Learn what may be coming later on.

I recently found an article on *Quanta Magazine's* website, "A Power Law Keeps the Brain's Perceptions Balanced," which talks about recent research that shows a "mathematical relationship in the brain's representations of sensory information." In essence, it shows that neural activity patterns are as "detailed, or high-dimensional, as they can possibly be without becoming fractal, or non-smooth." While the article speaks more about how this research would be applicable to artificial intelligence, I would be interested to find out if the results from that research would be the same for autistic brains. If not, it may give researchers in the future another avenue to pursue to further our collective understanding of autism.

Every person with autism is unique and not everything you learn may apply in your situation. You may even disagree with some of what you read, because it hasn't been your experience. It's okay to be skeptical at times, just keep learning.

You may even disagree with me now, but I believe it is important to remember that the purpose of educating yourself is to help those with autism, not to place blame for the condition or look for a magic cure. Neither is helpful to the situation, and both take your focus away from understanding how you can best support, help, guide, and interact with those who have challenges from ASD in the here and now.

Observe and Analyze

This is an ongoing activity. What behaviors manifest under what conditions? Is the child overtired or ill? Is it only at school or also at home? Is it only with certain people? What sensory stressors are present? And so on. Pay attention to the child's cues. Note body language and changes in behavior or speech. You may need to keep a notebook to track what you observe.

I cannot stress enough how important it is to understand how autism affects the one specific individual. This understanding affects how you approach your plans and goals, your patience, and your handling of stressful situations. Know that as someone with autism grows in one or more competencies, his/her autism may begin to manifest in other new ways that may or may not need to be addressed. Everyone, autistic or neurotypical, changes as they grow, mature, and have more life experiences. You can better aid an autistic child if you remain observant and sensitive to those changes.

Another important thing to remember is that not everything a person says or does has to do with autism. Their autism doesn't define who they are; it is just one, though admittedly large, aspect of the person. In many instances, being aware of what is typical child development or part of their personality and what can be attributed to autistic traits will change how you handle a situation or discussion. In April's case, not doing her homework in eighth grade was not an unexpected teenage challenge, but her autism exacerbated the situation. With autism, she doesn't have the luxury of going too far down a side path. Being able to differentiate and understand the interaction between the two was critical in how we chose to handle it and in how April viewed herself afterwards.

Know Your Goals

Short-term and long-term. What competencies are you trying to develop? What areas of growth need to have the highest priority?

It is a normal and instinctive reaction to go with as many supports as you can to help a child, especially if you are that child's parent. Depending on the child's age and challenges, it may the most appropriate action at the time. However, remember one long-term goal is to be able to reduce supports to those that can be reasonably accommodated after the child reaches legal age, though it may be years before you can do so. Another is that the autistic individual will be able to advocate for himself/herself.

It takes longer for some competencies to be mastered, so start as early as you can. In April's case, it took over a decade to be able to ask a teacher for help with schoolwork verbally and do it without anxiety.

Plan

This is different from the goals. Planning is for specific situations. Planning is determining whether or not a child requires their name called first before asking him/her a question. Planning is whether or not a child needs to take quizzes and tests in a smaller classroom. Planning is having an exit strategy if you are unsure if an autistic person will be able to cope with sensory stressors, such as the laser light show we attended with April. Planning is whether or not you take two vehicles to a large party and deciding who will stay or go if the autistic individual needs to leave significantly sooner than the rest of your family. Planning is ensuring you have MP3 players, electronic devices, a special comfort item, or whatever helps someone cope in the larger neurotypical world with you before you enter that world with your autistic individual. In our family, April is quite capable of packing her own go-bag, but I've learned that I need to keep extra earbuds with me when we'll be out somewhere where we can't stop and buy them easily, in case someone's earbuds become unusable.

Planning is also in the smaller steps you take to achieve a goal. One of our goals was to have the children be able to stay home alone without fear when they were old enough, so we developed a plan with incremental steps. Planning for what may be a major stressor, such as the changes of puberty and future female reproductive health appointments, may need to start years in advance.

As an air traffic controller, I was used to planning for all eventualities, so this is a natural activity for me. John, not so much. In a family, you may find one parent is better suited for the planning portion. However, you do need to communicate with one another about the plan. In our case, I've found that John is good at spotting potential pitfalls or has helpful ideas to add once an initial plan is developed so we can adjust the plan accordingly before we need to implement it.

Aim for Flexibility

This applies to all things. You need to be flexible with your plans and goals to a certain extent. You will believe you have reached one step in your overall plan or goal, but suddenly, you're looking at a different behavior that is an offshoot of the first in some way or something you never realized was an issue and have to adjust your plans or goals to compensate. It has been my experience that it's two steps forward, one step back. And the cycle will repeat several times before the soundwaves settle into the new refrain of the person's overall calmer ASD music.

Flexibility means being able to leave an event early because it becomes too much for your autistic companion to cope. Flexibility means planning your day or errands around another's needs. Flexibility means realizing that maybe the child needs some time off from all the plans to "just be."

The stereotype that autistic people cannot be flexible is untrue. Some people with autism do require more structure than others. In April's case, she requires more structure at school and dislikes changes in those schedules. However, at home, we discovered that she needs unstructured time to relax before addressing things like homework or chores. It's during those relaxed, unstructured times that she routinely reveals the best, funniest, and most engaging parts of her personality.

If you over-structure an autistic person's day, you may find that you're not allowing them time to decompress or to build a greater tolerance for flexibility in their own lives. Even though it sounds counterintuitive, you may have to plan your flexibility if the child has a great need for structure now to build his/her tolerance for flexibility in the future.

This is one of those instances where I am glad that we were not aware of April's autism earlier, because I might have gone overboard with structure before I knew better. Flexibility is very important to John, for reasons too many to enumerate. For the children, I like to have some structure, because I do think they need it, but I am not anal retentive about it. With our work schedules we had to be flexible, which meant our children had to learn to live with it to a certain extent.

With April, I think my hospitalization when she was young, but old enough to remember, created a fear that I might not be coming home at all if I was not home at bedtime. It was a normal childhood fear that her autism exacerbated, creating a constant, low level of daily stress that none of us, including her, realized went far beyond those first few months afterwards.

Advocate

Until a child is able to do so for himself/herself, advocate for them. As a parent, you are their primary advocate; you know your child best. I have also advocated within our school district and county for changes in how they approach IEPs and training so that parents are better aware and informed of what long-term goals are needed for a child after high school.

However, if you are an educational professional, you should be advocating to the parent(s) as well. Perhaps you send information to a parent about training that might help the child or the parent. Advocacy comes in many forms. In our case, Miss Lisa advocated for April by suggesting an evaluation for early intervention. Sunny advocated for her for a set break time in the afternoons. Hope advocated for her by suggesting a change in Language Arts classes.

Work as a Team

We are part of a team working towards successful outcomes for an autistic child. It is not solely the parents' responsibility, nor is it solely the school's responsibility.

The child should be part of the team as age appropriate. I don't mean as they turn fourteen years old as required by IDEA, but when they are younger. You should be asking his/her input on how the team can help them solve specific problems. Yes, you may be guiding them early on because they are not yet able to understand or articulate what they need. But it's only one step on the road to self-advocacy, so the child needs to be part of the process. It's not only his/her daily life and coping strategies we are attempting to improve, but also his/her future life without all the supports he/she counts on now.

Some behaviors will be more evident at school, some at home, some in both settings. Neither parents nor the educators have all the right answers all of the time. We need to work together and keep the child's best interests first and foremost as the priority.

Communicate and Listen

Communicate with your partner. Communicate with the educators. Communicate with the parents. Above all, communicate with the child. Communication is a two-way street and includes truly listening to one another.

The teamwork portion will not be nearly as effective if people do not communicate with and understand one another. I have seen marriages deteriorate because the parents of an autistic child were unable to communicate and listen to one another. One parent may be further along the path to acceptance of autism in their lives than the other. Parents may disagree on what autism means for their child. There may be other issues not related to autism involved. Regardless of whether parents are married or not, they still have to work for the best interests of their child, who needs the love and support of both parents to have the most successful outcomes.

Parents need to communicate with the school's educators and support personnel about goals, plans, and home issues that may affect the child in the school environment. And they need to listen to educators if they bring up a concern they are observing at school. This does not mean the parents have to agree with the educator's assessments or proposed solutions if any are offered, but they do need to listen with an open mind and not default to "not my child" or "I thought that was 'fixed.'"

Educators need to communicate with parents, not only about what they are observing in the school environment, but also to acknowledge a parent's communication and to offer potential solutions if they have any. I know of educators who believe they know a child's needs best because they have a degree in education. Parents know their child best; they live with them. The parents are the team leads until a child can do it for himself/herself, not just because they are the parents, but because they have the most information coming in from a variety of people, especially at the higher grades; they're the ones who will most likely see a pattern developing before anyone else.

And communicating with the child is key to understanding what the underlying issues are. While observation and analysis will get you further along, once a child can begin to articulate what the problem might be, you will get where you want to go faster. If I had tried to guess what was happening when April's seventh grade paraprofessional was out of work or just assumed it was a teenage developmental issue similar to the one we later experienced in eighth grade, I would have been wrong. She was able to tell me why she wasn't bringing her assignments home, even if she hadn't been able to ask for help with the problem sooner.

If you've made a mistake with the child, own it and communicate it to him/her with a sincere apology. Many autistic children have difficulties understanding that sustained perfection is unattainable. Model the behavior you want them to learn.

You want to communicate your feelings to your child, but carefully. When he/she is calm, it's more than okay for them to see you sad or angry about something so you can teach them that the more difficult emotions aren't bad. Let them see different constructive ways to deal with those emotions. Just be sure that you aren't making it about their autism.

Never communicate that you are sad or angry about your child's autism. You do not want them to feel bad about a very large part of themselves. You can, however, tell them that you're sad they have to struggle sometimes, and that you wish you had the power to make the challenges easier or less stressful for them. That honest reframing of the emotion makes it about their distress as someone you love deeply, not about who they are and always will be.

Another key point is to listen to yourself and your instincts. If something feels like it's a wrong approach to take with the child, it probably is. If you are keeping an open mind, have educated yourself, and truly know the child, your instincts may be letting you know that a path is the wrong one to take.

Keep It Matter of Fact

When communicating with an autistic individual about something important or potentially stress-inducing, it is best to state the information in a matter-of-fact manner and tone to reduce the chances of a fight-or-flight emotional reaction. Depending on the person, you may have to preface your remarks with a statement that heads off an automatic hamster on the wheel response.

For instance, if I call April unexpectedly from an activity at home and ask her to sit with me, I usually have to preface whatever I want to talk about with something like "I'm not mad; you're not in trouble. There is just something I would like to talk to you about." Many times, April's instinctual hamster on the wheel reaction is to think she did something wrong and she's in trouble, even if she knows she hasn't done or said anything that could be an issue.

If it is an important issue, like explaining the autism diagnosis or an unexpected change coming in their lives (like family members coming to live with us), keeping it factual helps to maximize your chances that it will not become as big an issue for the autistic individual in the future. Remember how the hippocampus stores the memories and reminds us which emotional reactions are "congruent with our mood?" You want your important information to be associated with calmness or even fun, if it's appropriate to fit it in, when they recall the conversation later. You want the child's hamster on the wheel to stay sleeping.

Practice Patience

This can sometimes be a difficult one, especially during an unexpected meltdown. But it is important. Your calm can aid in reducing an autistic individual's recovery time from a meltdown.

Patience is also needed because you're in it for the long haul; this is a marathon, not a sprint. Achieving successful outcomes takes years. It is not unusual for you and the child to become frustrated along the way. Remind the child of how far they have come; you'll be reminding yourself at the same time. Let him or her know how proud you are of their efforts and the progress they've made so far. Encourage them to be proud of themselves and their efforts. If you are not normally a patient person, find ways to cultivate it within yourself. It's not easy; believe me, I know. But it really does make the journey easier.

Forgive

Forgive yourself, especially if you lose patience once in a while. You are human; you cannot be a perfect parent or educator 100% of the time. We have stressors too.

Forgive yourself for the mistakes you will make along the way. You are human; do the best you can with what you have.

And try to forgive others for their ignorance.

Compromise

There will be times you will need to compromise. There are competing needs in each family's life. Your child is your priority, but if you have other children, they too are a priority. As is your marriage. And your extended family. And your jobs. And you. And so on. Find a balance as best you can. Sometimes the scales tip one way or another. And go back to forgiving yourself if you sometimes muck it up.

As in any parent-child relationship, you will be compromising there as well. Not every child's personality or emotional needs closely match your own, regardless of autism. As in the case of April's comfort level with physical affection, she and I have found a compromise that works for both of us.

Create a Safe Space

If you can, try to create a safe space for a child to retreat to when they feel the need. At school it may be a sensory area in the support classroom or a meditation area such as we have in our high school. At home, it may a corner of a less-traveled room with pillows, special stuffed or sensory toys, and a covering to filter the light to your child's preferences. Don't forget sound; headphones and a MP3 player with music or calming sounds might be needed to block out other household noises.

For the home, do your best to have it set up based on your child's specific needs as well as yours. By that I mean, if your child's coping strategies currently include some activity where you would worry he or she may sustain injuries (yes, I know you're working on it!), you have to have the space where you can easily keep an eye on your child without intruding unless you need to keep your child safe. Stock it with items that normally work to calm your child as he/she learns to self-soothe and self-regulate.

Push

Unless you are the type of person who would throw a child in the deep end of a pool to teach them how to swim, push the child outside his/her comfort zones, just as you would a neurotypical child. Carefully plan those gentle pushes. Plan small, incremental steps.

You want the child to be stretching the boundaries of his/her comfort zone a little at a time, not crashing through them. Imagine a toy on a shelf that the child wants, but that shelf is just out of reach. You want the shelf just low enough so that if the child stands on his/her tiptoes, they can get the toy.

Build on the child's successes, and positively reinforce them. For a number of years, April was uncomfortable ordering her own food at restaurants or paying for an item she wanted without an adult to help her. April isn't quite at the point of being comfortable enough to try going into a store alone to make a purchase, but she is happy to go with her brother without John or me. Now that she has been successful in expanding her boundaries, she may be ready to go in without her brother someday soon.

Presume competence, but remember that it's okay for the child to fail on occasion. Making mistakes is part of life. For parents, it's a natural instinct to want to protect your child from all pain, but you have to allow your child the experiences of failing and trying again. Autism is not a get-out-of-jail-free card; you would be doing a grave disservice to the child if you parent or educate in that fashion.

Reflect and Revise

It is easy to get caught up in the day-to-day. It is even easier to look at how far you still have to go and get discouraged. If you are feeling that way, the first thing you should do is carve out some quiet time for yourself and reflect back. See how far you've already traveled on the path. Sometimes you only have to go back in time a few months to identify progress. Other times, you may have to go further back. If something isn't working for the child and you've given it lots of time, look for other options and revise your plans based on what you know now. Sometimes it only requires a small tweak in a plan—like adding a Help card to a Break card; other times it may require wholesale changes.

I know a family with an autistic child who chose to home school when the child was older because the social stressors were becoming too much for him/her. I know another family who homeschooled for a year after elementary school because they felt their child was not yet ready for the transition to a new school. When the child did return to the public-school system after the year, the transition was a positive one. There is no one-size-fits-all path.

Be Creative

You will find you need to think outside of the box at times to meet the child's needs and usher them along the path. Sometime it's rewards, like Sunny wanting to paint April's fingernails. Sometimes it's thinking of solutions that meet a child's needs, like the pocketbook with a pocket on the outside for a cherished stress reliever. Sometimes it's thinking of analogies or reframing an issue that your child can understand in order to open up an alternate pathway of thought and to get beyond a block caused by an emotional reaction. In April's case, as she became older and needed a break, there were times she would refuse to take one because she worried about her peers knowing. Her hamster on the wheel would start with thoughts that her classmates would think, "How come she gets a break and I don't? What makes her so special?" When reframed to When reframed to asking to go to the restroom and taking a sneaky break, she was provided a pathway to bypass her hamster completely, because there was no emotional reaction in her mind associated with needing to use the restroom. She knew no one even noticed restroom breaks; everyone takes them.

Develop a Thick Skin

The neurotypical world isn't always kind to those who are perceived as different. Bystanders may openly judge your child or your parenting skills. Try to remember they are not important to you; your child is. Those bystanders have not walked in your shoes nor your child's, and, quite frankly, have absolutely no idea how hard your child works to get through some days. Do not take their words to heart. Their uninformed judgments do not reflect negatively on your family, only on themselves.

Accept

Accept that the child has autism and will always have autism. How much that autism will affect his/her life and life choices will be determined by how much progress they can make in managing their sensory overload and emotions. Each autistic person is different, just as each neurotypical person is different. You can't force the progress; you can only guide and support it.

Accept that the child may always have a need that visually identifies him/her as a little different to the neurotypical world. If it hurts no one and isn't unsanitary, accept it and protect it fiercely if the individual needs you to.

In April's case, Torchic is necessary now. If the opportunity presents itself in the future for a smaller, less visible item that would also fit her needs, then, yes, I would encourage—but never force—her to transition for the reason that there would be less opportunities for outsiders to erroneously base their assumptions on her capabilities solely by his presence.

However, if Torchic ends up being part of April's daily life until she is ninety years old and eventually gets buried with her, that's also fine with me. If the choices are Torchic is with her and she is confident navigating the neurotypical world to achieve her dreams or forcing her to leave him behind and her being anxious and stress-filled, the choice is clear to me—Torchic stays.

In Beckett's case, his happy stim may look odd to some, but he needs it for whatever reason. If he needs it into adulthood, then hopefully, his happiness will also be spread to others; we all need more uninhibited delight in our lives. If it doesn't bother Beckett, then it doesn't bother me. In my mind, it is no different than football players doing their own happy touchdown dances in the end zone; Beckett just finds more opportunities to express his happiness. In truth, I would miss seeing Beckett's happy stim if he stopped. When he does it, I cannot help but smile at his unbridled joy.

Love

Love your child for who he or she is now and is becoming. Love their efforts during difficult circumstances. Love yourself for your efforts during difficult circumstances. Find ways to express your love in ways your child can tolerate, appreciate, and understand.

CHAPTER 19

COVID-19 & CONTINUITY OF LEARNING

Abruptly changing world.

Down is up, up is down

Right is left, left is right.

Unforeseen transition.

Together we face

The new day and night.

THIS CHAPTER IS a late addition to the book. You see, I was waiting for our tax refund to be able to afford the final edit before moving quickly to publishing when the Coronavirus (COVID-19) changed all our lives. We went from bus and work routines, family income being a little tight as we recovered from the expenses of John's illness last year, and prompting about homework and chores and encouraging social interaction to waking up late, everyone home all day, worrying about the cost of groceries, figuring out how to continue learning curriculum at home and social distancing.

As I write this, we're still in the midst of trying to complete ninth grade from home and facing an uncertain transition to tenth grade and what changes that might entail. So many things I mentioned in the previous chapter, What I've Learned, have come into play in recent weeks.

Educate Yourself

Our entire family has been keeping up with the news and research on COVID-19. John, my mother, and I are in high-risk categories as are so many others, and we want to ensure that we understand what needs to be done to keep as many people as possible safe. I also want to have a sense of what schooling might look like next school year so that I can prepare the children for that transition since it's unlikely we will have a vaccine or anti-viral treatment tested and produced by that time.

Observe and Analyze

Both children have had periods of not finishing their schoolwork. I am spending a lot of time trying to determine if it's related to certain subjects, activities, feeling unmotivated because of the change in circumstances, or some teenage developmental stage that I just haven't recognized yet.

Several weeks in, I printed out a list of all their missing assignments and told them I expected them completed by the end of the day. April went through the list and wrote why she hadn't completed her work. As I looked at what she had written, I realized, in every instance, the first step necessary was for her to ask for assistance, either from me or a teacher.

Beckett, on the other hand, has shown some behaviors that lead me to believe that we need to have him evaluated when it's safe to do so. His inability to ask for assistance and difficulties with emotional regulation and executive function combined with a recent incident of hair pulling when upset make me wonder if he has been able to successfully cope or mask ASD until the combined stressors of puberty, the pandemic, and numerous life changes all at once made it too difficult. If that is the case, then our unexpected time at home has had a benefit—he'll get additional support he may need going forward. While he hasn't shown any issues with social awareness to date, it is possible that we have missed them or they are slight enough to be manageable without support.

Know Your Goals

One goal is to keep everyone safe and healthy, both physically and emotionally. The other is to finish ninth grade and continue to make some sort of forward progress with April's ability to cope with all aspects of her autism. Our focus has temporarily shifted to self-advocacy and executive function, since that is what she requires most for the continuity of learning from home. Of course, our goals for Beckett are similar.

Plan

John and I have begun speaking to the children about the various scenarios of what school might look like in the fall to prepare them as much as possible. We have also discussed whether or not to send the children back to school if we don't agree with whatever plan the district puts in place.

John and I updated our wills and ensured that important information is readily available. We also have made plans on where and how to quarantine a member of the family if one of us becomes ill with COVID-19. We've discussed how to limit potential spread in the household by using disposable dinnerware, silverware, etc. for anyone who might be ill as well as covering air ducts in our home if it becomes necessary.

Aim for Flexibility

We had to be flexible when school was cancelled for two weeks initially and as we waited for a continuity of learning plan to be developed, before it was ultimately decided that school facilities would remain closed for the remainder of the school year. Obviously, we had to adjust our lives to eliminate physical social interaction, which meant no family gatherings with the extended family or trips just for fun. Attempting to determine what works best for each child to motivate them to finish their assignments in a timely fashion has also required a lot of flexibility.

The children have had to be flexible since not all their teachers have been using the particular online platform endorsed by the school district. Not all of the educators organize the assignments and information in the same way or communicate clearly in writing.

The educators have had to be flexible, not only in their lesson planning, but in determining where and when a student may need extra assistance. Since they don't have the ability to note body language while teaching, they have lost a tool in their toolkit.

Advocate

I have already initiated a request to have Beckett evaluated by the school district. I have sent questions to our school board about various scenarios for the fall to ensure they consider a number of different options.

Work as a Team

Sam has been reaching out to me regularly, offering whatever assistance he can to help April during this time. Teachers have been responsive to messages from the children as well as from myself.

Communicate and Listen

April and Beckett have expressed their fears that they may catch COVID-19 and infect John and me. Since John is the only one who may have to work, we decided that he is the only one to do the shopping and risk exposure. Seeing their parents be smart and consistent with this plan as well as John immediately washing and disinfecting items, including doorknobs, after being in public seems to have reduced our children's fears to a manageable level.

I have communicated to the children that I dislike nagging them about their schoolwork. I have also told them that I do not want them to have to repeat ninth grade when there is no legitimate reason not to do the work assigned.

I have observed and listened to April's responses as we have worked to find ways to make learning from home easier on all of us. I noted that if I tried to keep her to a schedule or encouraged her to use her Help card, she resisted strongly. In her mind, school is different from home and we can't mix certain supports. I can't change that emotional reaction, so I have to work around it.

Keep It Matter of Fact
John and I have remained calm and straightforward with our children during all of our discussions about what other changes we may face due to the Coronavirus.

Practice Patience
Patience and understanding have been necessary in dealing with a previously unimagined situation. Knowing the children have their own fears about health and the future, some which they may not yet have communicated to us, John and I are doing our best to give them a little extra leeway and keep the lines of communication open.

Forgive
I have had to forgive myself for getting frustrated and feeling overwhelmed at times. As a parent, it's much easier to prompt to finish a couple homework assignments than it is being responsible for ensuring all schoolwork is accomplished.

Compromise
Being teenagers, April and Beckett want to stay up late and sleep in late. John and I have compromised by letting them do so, so long as they check in on their schoolwork by noon. Their teachers are available online from 10am to 2pm for questions, and we want to ensure that if the children have questions, they ask them during that time. We have told the kids that it is not reasonable, fair, or courteous to expect their teachers to respond to their needs during other times; their teachers have their own families and personal responsibilities too.

Push

Beckett has attempted to emotionally separate himself from the family a couple times thus far as he tries to find his path through puberty and pandemic-related changes. I've given him space, but keep gently pushing reminders that he is not allowed to emotionally distance himself from the family as a long-term solution.

Reflect and Revise

This has been necessary regularly as I try to find what works for each child. I have come to the realization that schedules won't work for either Beckett or April. I have tried twenty minutes of work, followed by a twenty-minute break. I have also tried using colored paper as a visual reminder that when green is up on the wall, each should be working on Language Arts. Neither of which has worked for us.

Be Creative

Given April's resistance to using school supports at home, I came up with a different solution. I made a Help poster, listing the various areas in which she might need assistance with schoolwork; the major categories are supplies, technology, directions, "I Don't Understand," and other. Each category has subcategories with more specific items that might be an issue, such as having to message a teacher or needing printer ink under *technology*. There is a Post-it note with an arrow she can move to point to the item she needs help with.

The poster hangs across from where April sits at the laptop that she received for Christmas. I hope that it will be an avenue for her to use her prefrontal cortex instead of her amygdala when she needs assistance. She really likes the poster, but I honestly don't believe she'll end up using it to communicate with me. I think she'll find it easier to just tell me what she needs now that she has a backup plan in place to reduce her anxiety.

Develop a Thick Skin

Since I am now Mom, counselor, teacher, and sometimes drill sergeant, I am not always popular with my teenage children. Fortunately, our home and yard are large enough that any of us can find privacy if it's wanted or needed.

Accept

All of us have accepted that we have no real control over the Coronavirus. All any of us can do is deal with the resultant emotions about the situation and control our own actions in doing our part not to spread it if it visits our household.

Love

We are loving each other during these difficult circumstances. That's all any of us can do.

Under normal circumstances, John and I would not have had this extra time with our children at this stage in their lives. While I don't like the reasons why we have had it, I plan to take advantage of it and enjoy all of us reaping whatever benefits we can from the situation.

April is socializing more with me; we're just having various conversations throughout the day. We're giggling, teasing, and connecting more regularly than we seem to do during normal school routines. Part of that may be that she doesn't require time to decompress after a school day. No matter the reason, I love it.

She made an observation early on that our air hugs and kisses would have looked strange to others before the pandemic, but maybe now we'll be trendsetters. She may be right, and it's positive that something that aids her will not appear unusual to the neurotypical world.

The children's stay-at-home sleep schedules more closely match their teenage circadian rhythms. Both children seem better rested and calmer overall than usual. Since they are sleeping in, not eating breakfast as often, don't have the opportunities for extra servings of French fries at lunch, don't have nearly as many chances to have fast food, and doing their twenty minutes of physical activity per day for physical education, Beckett has dropped some excess weight and is looking trimmer. He looks and feels better. Even April's face seems to have thinned a little.

I have been occasionally talking each child through making their favorite snacks. I have been letting them do all the measuring, mixing, and cooking with me available to guide them. John has been finding more things for them to do outside to help beyond mowing the lawn. Both are learning new skills and seem less resistant to learning them because they are well rested and relaxed.

Thus far, we have been fortunate that we have been doing well physically and mentally and able to find the good in the situation. While I may sometimes wonder how this will affect April's progress in some areas, we simply have to adapt and focus on other areas in the meantime and believe it will all work out as it should in the end.

CHAPTER 20

DREAMS

Our dreams are for the essence of you.
Your dreams are yet to be seen.
We love you tomorrow and today.
Whomever you are, whatever you do
May your heart stay full and your intellect keen.
We're here if you ever lose your way.

I THINK ANYONE who is becoming a parent has their own visions of what parenthood will look like. I honestly thought I would be a much stricter parent than I am. I was going to be the mom who did all sorts of crafts with my kids on a regular basis. Our home would be insanely decorated for every holiday. Our children would come home from school every few weeks to the smell of freshly baked homemade cookies. In Mary Poppins style, I would make chores fun. I imagined our household would be the one where all the kids would hang out downstairs in the family room, doing whatever teenagers do and eating us out of house and home. I would know all their friends and those friends would be comfortable coming to me for advice if they needed it.

I imagined April and I playing with each other's hair during her childhood years, giggling. I imagined us talking about our loves and angsts and anything else over Doritos and Dr. Pepper, a tradition Auntie Karen and I had had as teenagers. I also imagined our children telling me everything that happened during their respective days.

I imagined that our children would love to read books as much as I do—voraciously. I hoped they would love music and play the piano, as well as sing. We would take them to museums every couple of months and explore, learning all kinds of new things together. We would be regular theater-goers, and they would love the theater as much as I do. We would go camping with tents and maybe we'd fish. John imagined coaching baseball and softball and our son possibly playing football like he did. He hoped one of them might want to become an excavator, and he could teach them all he knows about the career.

The reality is I'm a marshmallow more often than not with our children and pick and choose the battles I think are worth fighting. I was too exhausted most of the time to handle the crafts on a regular basis, especially after cleaning up some of the messes involving glitter. Again, I was too exhausted to do much decorating for any holiday other than Christmas, and that is on a much smaller scale than I had imagined. Freshly baked homemade cookies also got added to the *exhausted* heap. Uhh, chores fun? No real success with that one. Our children aren't interested in having friends over regularly; they're happy with each other and electronic communication. I do, however, know their friends and most of their classmates from my years as PTA-mom-extraordinaire. The jury is still out on whether any of them would come to me for advice though.

April is impatient when I brush her hair but may let me blow dry it occasionally. While she does love Doritos and Dr. Pepper and will share those with me, it has never become a tradition signifying emotional sharing between us. And now that puberty is here, getting information from our children about their days can sometimes be a long, protracted affair.

Beckett and April did love reading books for a while, but have fallen out of the habit once they started spending more time on the computer and their phones. They do love music, but only dabble with the piano. April has a beautiful voice but refuses to sing. Museum visits happen maybe twice a year, and if they aren't interactive, the kids rush through them unless they come to an exhibit that really interests them—I have to take pictures of the placards so I can take the time to read them later. We don't get to the theater often, but the kids do love to attend. The closest we've gotten to camping is sleeping in a minivan rental in a cemetery— long story there—and renting a cabin at Sebago Lake. Since the kids come find John or me if there is a stinkbug or spider in the house so we can take care of it, I think it is safe to say worms on a hook are not their cup of tea. You already know how baseball and softball worked out, and while Beckett is built like a linebacker, none of us foresees football in his future. April has always loved to play in the dirt, but has no interest in excavation as a career.

All of those imaginings of what life would be like were mine or John's, not Beckett's or April's. It's what we wanted for *us*. My releasing of those particular dreams is less about autism in our lives and more about the reality of life and the knowledge that most of them probably would not have happened even if both children were firmly on the neurotypical side of the equation.

I remember once seeing a video of a mom of a younger ASD child with challenges that far exceed April's. The woman was talking about how you experience grief and mourn for the child you thought you would have before you move on to loving the child in your life. Maybe it's the semi-convoluted path we have traveled on our journey with its different challenges, but I have personally never experienced that grief. I haven't shaken my fist at fate, thought it was unfair, or wondered "Why her?" None of that. I have cried, yes, but not because April is autistic. Just as I wouldn't cry if she is transgender, asexual, or any other label considered outside the societal norm. Her autism is part of who she is, just as her beautiful blue eyes and sexuality are.

I cried for my little girl's pain, anxiety, and struggles before I knew she had autism, and if there were a magic wand that could take away her autism in the future, I would still cry for my little girl's pain, anxiety, and struggles, no matter what circumstances created them. It may be a fine distinction for some, but it's how I feel.

⤚

However, I admit I had a period where I did not own the autism in our lives publicly, instead only sharing with those I was closest to or had a need to know. It wasn't shame. It wasn't denial. It wasn't anger. It wasn't grief. I did not own it because I did not understand yet what it meant for our family's journey.

I felt vastly unprepared for the circumstances. *These were my babies.* I needed time to research, digest, reflect, and deal with the mom guilt that my ignorance may have created more anxiety for our children and made their trek along our path more difficult than it needed to be. Once I had done all of those things and I felt I understood how the path was going to continue to twist and turn—with unexpected switchbacks, roadblocks, and uneven terrain—I discovered that I could own it easily. Any path in life has unexpected obstacles, but now I could plan for the proper equipment for our journey and read the markers of the landscape in front of us significantly better.

You see, my most heartfelt dreams for our children, the dreams I have *for them*, have not changed because of autism. I still want them to become happy, healthy, whole, kind, successful adults who love themselves and others. I want them to be responsible, trustworthy, and hard-working. I want them to feel pride in their accomplishments and know their own self-worth. I want them to own, learn, and grow from their mistakes and missteps. I want them to have confidence that they can keep getting up and trying their best each time life or circumstance knocks them down. I want them to stay true to their own moral code and stand up for what they believe to be right, for themselves and for others. I want them to be critical thinkers who can still understand a differing viewpoint. I want them never to forget the value of family and to make family a priority in their lives. I want them to enjoy life, laugh often, and never stop learning. I want them never to doubt how much John and I love them and carry that security with them forever.

What has changed is that achieving the dreams I have for our children now requires a different sometimes more difficult path because of autism. I have had to become a more educated parent in a variety of disciplines. I have had to develop a greater level of patience and understanding within myself than I might have otherwise. My priorities on how to best guide, push, and support our children getting from point A to point B have reduced to smaller increments and sometimes have to be planned years in advance in painstaking detail. I have had to become even more creative than I was when I was childless. But that's okay; having children is not just about their personal growth, it is also about ours. I have always worked hard and done what is necessary to achieve my dreams; in my mind, the effort is worth the rewards. The stakes are just higher for me now with these dreams for our children.

I never dreamed of having perfect children—children who do no wrong, experience no setbacks, or succeed first try at everything. Actually, perfect children would frighten me, and I know I would be certain there was something seriously wrong with them and drag them off to the nearest psychiatrist.

But here's the thing, Beckett and April, with all their human imperfections, *are* the perfect children for John and me. Who they are and who they are becoming brings us great joy every day.

CHAPTER 21

FINAL THOUGHTS

Love. A girl and a boy.
Obstacles. Challenges galore.
You. Wonder and joy.
Effort. Confidence and more.

I AM PROFOUNDLY grateful that my childhood premonition was correct. I can't imagine my life without either of our children, nor would I want to. The joy they bring to our lives is immeasurable. And I know that the journey is easier for both of them than it might have been without the love, support, and understanding of his/her sibling.

While I may wish I could have reduced the daily struggles and anxiety to save them some pain, if there were something that could take it all away, I don't think I would want that. I could not take the risk that either Beckett or April would end up being anyone other than each is now. As I watch these delightful, wonderful beings learn and grow into their future adult selves, I am continually amazed that John and I haven't completely bungled the process somewhere along the way.

I am also grateful that I gave birth later in life. Knowing how I was when I was younger and still had enough energy, I might have gone overboard—looking or hoping for faster results. I would have increased our children's stress and possibly damaged my marriage. Instead, by the time I had the twins, my life experiences had already taught me and reinforced that people, regardless of age or ability, learn at their own pace and get there when they get there—if they ever do. I had learned that if you push a person too hard and too fast, you do more harm than good. I had become more relaxed about milestones, so long as I could see growth.

Recently John and I were talking about the challenges of parenting a child with high-functioning autism and how, for the most part, we have found it easy to adjust. Yes, some days are more difficult, but, overall, we don't resent or mind the changes we have had to make as parents to support our children. However, there is one aspect that I intensely abhor about April's autism: her self-confidence is so often the casualty. Our daughter is bright, creative, articulate, funny, and caring. Yet, when her hamster on the wheel starts furiously churning its feet, she has difficulty remembering all that is wonderful about herself and that there is so much more good about her than needs improvement.

How much of our children's autistic traits are exacerbated by the genes they inherited from John and me or by the environment they live in? Obviously, all of their DNA came from us, but John is a well-practiced procrastinator. How much of their difficulties with executive function stem from that rather than autism?

And monotropic mindset, the ability to focus narrowly and difficulty transitioning out of that state, how much of that comes from me rather than autism? John likes to tease me about my rabbit holes and, thankfully, has always supported me when I dive into them. Friends, family, and former coworkers are aware of my tendency to do more than is necessary, in greater detail, and doing it all in less time than most other people. It is not unusual for me to get so involved in something interesting to me that I ignore all but the most important tasks needed in my life.

The most recent example is writing this book; it only took me a few weeks to write the first rough draft, but I ignored most of the household duties during that time. If it didn't involve me picking up the kids so they weren't stranded somewhere or throwing all the laundry into the washing machine once a week, I let it go and John picked up the slack. Our morning and bedtime routines remained sacrosanct though. When I go down one of my rabbit holes, even taking something out of the freezer to thaw for dinner seems like too much of a distraction for me and it is not unusual for me to forget to eat lunch.

I also occasionally wonder if autism is one of the first steps of the next stage of human evolution, preparing our species for using more of our brains effectively as the demands on said brains increase. I'll never know the answers to these types of questions, but it doesn't mean I don't think about them.

I see the world around me acting strangely at times. People want to be understood and accepted as they are—people who live, love, grieve, and have something worthwhile to contribute to their own little patch of community—no different from anyone else. And they should be understood and accepted. Yet there also seems to be a growing excitement to label ourselves to highlight our uniqueness. Male, female, non-binary, transgender. Caucasian, African-American, Indian, Asian. Democrat, Republican, Independent. Liberal, Conservative, Libertarian. Homosexual, heterosexual, asexual. Autistic, neurodivergent, neurotypical. And so on.

In my eyes, we are all unique and shouldn't have to define or label ourselves to prove that indisputable fact. I believe that the state of being unique is part of the human condition and, in essence, makes us no different from anyone else at our core. At times, I worry that all the labels confuse understanding and discourage acceptance at a deeper level—the opposite effect of what may be intended.

Sometimes I question what truly qualifies as different and why anyone really cares. April doesn't like large groups where she is expected to socialize. Introverts make up half of the world's population; that doesn't sound so different to me. Many of our society's greatest innovations, art, and field experts have come from those who have had intense, sometimes obsessive interests. At what point is an interest considered different or harmful? Is someone carrying a small plush toy really so different from someone counting rosary beads or wearing a lucky hat or shirt when a favorite sports team is playing if you consider that each of those items symbolize hope, support, calmness, or one's ability to cope during difficult moments?

Then I occasionally think, "What if?" What if we had decided to put the children in day care right away? What if we had recognized the signs earlier? What if April had exhibited more serious behaviors than "No, I don't know" with us? What if we had been properly informed earlier? Where would we be now? Would April's progress on some behaviors be significantly further along or would we have created more stress than necessary too early and instead exacerbated her fight-or-flight responses in those years?

In April's case, because of the way *her* autism manifests, I would like to believe that all that home time with us just accepting and adjusting to her cues benefited her in giving her a good baseline on what comfortable feels like for her. And she was interacting with her twin brother, so she was learning some social awareness, if in a smaller, more unintentional, protective bubble. She learned early on that flexibility could be fun, at least at home.

Beyond torturing myself occasionally with mom guilt, such questions are unanswerable and useless. What is, is. We can only do what we can from here.

There are certain worries that we, as parents, all share. Our child's health, their safety, their happiness, their future. Am I doing the right things for my child? Parents of special needs children have more worries on their plate. Will our child be able to live alone? Will our child be able to obtain and keep a job with his/her particular challenges? What will happen to our child if they are unable to live independently when we die? And the question "Am I doing the right things for my child?" in our darkest moments sometimes feels like a large, unnavigable abyss.

There are also certain moments of joy that we share as parents, ones we can all relate to. First smile, first laugh, first kiss, first words, first steps, first homerun or goal, a winning touchdown, a good grade in a difficult subject, high school graduation, becoming a grandparent, etc. For those of us living with autism, our paths are certainly rockier, and some of the joys experienced by parents of neurotypical children may never be ours.

But, in many ways, I think we experience more significant joys along the way, and we recognize them for the milestones they are because we know how difficult it was for our child to achieve them. Our specific joys may not be the same, but they are no less beautiful. Whether it's when your child first asked for help or was able to calm themselves without aid or was able to start a writing or math assignment without a prompt, you feel the same joy and pride as you did when they first laughed, even more so because of the effort involved. Straight As on a report card mean far less to us than our child being able to navigate transitions without distress. Our priorities shift and that is as it should be. From birth, our children are so much stronger than others may realize, coping with what they do just to make it through a day in a world and society that isn't designed for their brains.

If you have a child that isn't comfortable with hugs and kisses, you may sometimes secretly wish your child expressed physical affection more easily and without discomfort. But doesn't it feel wonderful when your child does reach out for your love and comfort when he/she needs it, even if it is lightly touching foreheads or fingertips? We appreciate and treasure every single one of those moments because they are rarer in our lives and when they happen, we *know* in every cell of our being that they are heartfelt.

Parents of neurotypical children may never truly understand how much you cherish such moments. I do. And there are a number of other parents on the journey living with autism that do too. We may not be traveling together, our paths may diverge wildly from one another's, or some of us may be ahead of you or behind you, but we understand our commonalities even if we are facing different challenges.

I wish you many joys and successes on your journey, whether you have autism, live with autism, or aid those with autism. Listen to, see, and enjoy the music...

RESOURCES

The following list is meant as a place for you to start if you are looking for more information on autism, and it is certainly not an all-encompassing list. Books are listed alphabetically by author; websites and blogs are listed alphabetically by organization name.

Not all of these resources may address your unique situation. I found some of these resources more helpful in our situation than others.

Books

Ariel, Cindy N. and Naseef, Robert A., editors. *Voices from the Spectrum: Parents, Grandparents, Siblings, People with Autism, and Professionals Share Their Wisdom.* Jessica Kingsley Publishers, 2005.

Barnett, Kristine. *The Spark: A Mother's Story of Nurturing, Genius, and Autism.* Random House, Reprint Edition, 2013.

Elder, Jennifer. *Different Like Me: My Book of Autism Heroes.* Jessica Kingsley Publishers, 2005.

Geither, Elise and Lisa Meeks. *Helping Students with Autism Spectrum Disorder Express their Thoughts and Knowledge in Writing: Tips and Exercises for Developing Writing Skills.* 1st ed., Jessica Kingsley Publishers, 2014.

Grandin, Temple. *The Autistic Brain: Thinking Across the Spectrum.* Mariner Books, Reprint Edition, 2013.

- *The Loving Push: How Parents and Professionals Can Help Spec-*

trum Kids Become Successful Adults. 1ˢᵗ ed., Future Horizons, 2016.

- *Thinking in Pictures, Expanded Edition: My Life with Autism.* Vintage, 2008.

- *Unwritten Rules of Social Relationships: Decoding Social Mysteries Through the Unique Perspectives of Autism: New Edition with Author Updates.* 2ⁿᵈ ed., Future Horizons, 2017.

Gray, Carol. *The New Social Story Book, Revised and Expanded 10th Anniversary Edition: Over 150 Social Stories that Teach Everyday Social Skills to Children with Autism or Asperger's Syndrome and their Peers.* Future Horizons, Revised Edition, 2012.

Higashida, Naoki. *The Reason I Jump: The Inner Voice of a Thirteen-Year-Old Boy with Autism.* Translated by K.A. Yoshida and David Mitchell, Random House Trade Paperbacks, Reprint Edition, 2016.

Hodgdon, Linda. *Top 60 Recommended Apps for Autism: Preschool through Adult (Technology for Autism Series Book 1).* 1ˢᵗ ed., Quirk Roberts Publishing, 2015.

Hoopman, Kathy. *All Cats Have Asperger Syndrome.* Jessica Kingsley Publishers, 2006.

McNamer, Tyler. *Population One: Autism, Adversity, and the Will to Succeed.* Avia, 2013.

Landa, Dr. Rebecca et al. *Chicken Soup for the Soul: Raising Kids on the Spectrum: 101 Inspirational Stories for Parents of Children with Autism and Asperger's.* Chicken Soup for the Soul, 2013.

Miles, Haley Morgan and Annellise Kolar. *The Hidden Curriculum and Other Everyday Challenges for Elementary-Age Children With High-Functioning Autism.* 2ⁿᵈ ed., AAPC Publishing, 2013.

Nichols, Shana et al. *Girls Growing Up on the Autism Spectrum: What Parents and Professionals Should Know About the Pre-Teen and Teenage Years.* Jessica Kingsley Publishers, 2009.

Notbohm, Ellen. *Ten Things Every Child with Autism Wishes You Knew, 3rd Edition: Revised and Updated.* Future Horizons, 2019.

Ozonoff, Sally PhD et al. *A Parent's Guide to High-Functioning Autism*

Spectrum Disorder, Second Edition: How to Meet the Challenges and Help Your Child Thrive. The Guilford Press, 2014.

Prizant, Barry M. PhD. *Uniquely Human: A Different Way of Seeing Autism.* Simon & Shuster, Reprint Edition, 2015.

Sabin, Ellen. *The Autism Acceptance Book: Being a Friend to Someone With Autism.* 1st ed., Watering Can Press, 2006.

Sicile-Kira, Chantal. *41 Things to Know about Autism (Good Things to Know).* Turner, 2010.

Silberman, Steve. *NeuroTribes: The Legacy of Autism and the Future of Neurodiversity.* 1st ed., April, 2015.

Toole, Janine PhD. *Six Minute Social Skills Workbook 1: Conversation Skills for Kids with Autism & Asperger's (Six-Minute Social Skills).* Happy Frog Press, 2017.

Verdick, Elizabeth and Elizabeth Reeve, M.D. *The Survival Guide for Kids with Autism Spectrum Disorders (And Their Parents).* Free Spirit Publishing, 2012.

Websites and Blogs

#ASDNext, www.asdnext.org.

"What are the 7 Senses?" *7 Senses Foundation*, www.7senses.org.au/what-are-the-7-senses.

"Autism." *American Psychiatric Association*, www.psychiatry.org/patients-families/autism/what-is-autism-spectrum-disorder.

"Autism (Autism Spectrum Disorder)." *American Speech-Language-Hearing Association*, www.asha.org/public/speech/disorders/Autism.

The Autism Services, Education, Resources and Training Collaborative (ASERT), www.paautism.org.

Autism Society, www.autism-society.org.

Autism Speaks, www.autismspeaks.org.

Kirby, Anne V. PhD. "Suicide risk in autism." *Autism Speaks*, 25 Jun. 2019, www.autismspeaks.org/expert-opinion/suicide-risk-autism.

Autistamatic, www.autistamatic.com.

"Social awareness increases demonstrate brain changing in adults with autism: Research shows virtual learning platform enhances neural health and social cognition in high-functioning adults on the spectrum." *Center for BrainHealth*, 28 Mar. 2018. www.sciencedaily.com/releases/2018/03/180328130733.htm.

Center for Parent Information and Resources, www.parentcenterhub.org.

"Executive Function and Self-Regulation." *Center on the Developing Child, Harvard University*, www.developingchild.harvard.edu/science/key-concepts/executive-function.

The Center on Secondary Education for Students with Autism Spectrum Disorder (CSESA), www.csesa.fpg.unc.edu.

"Autism Spectrum Disorder (ASD)." *Centers for Disease Control and Prevention*, www.cdc.gov/ncbddd/autism/facts.html.

The Children's Hospital of Philadelphia, Center for Autism Research, www.carautismroadmap.org.

College Autism Spectrum (CAS), www.collegeautismspectrum.com.

"Understanding the stress response; Chronic activation of this survival mechanism impairs health." *Harvard Medical School*, Mar. 2011, updated 1 May 2018, www.health.harvard.edu/staying-healthy/understanding-the-stress-response.

Skoyles, John R. "Autism, Context/Noncontext Information Processing, and Atypical Development." *Hindawi*, 6 Jun. 2011, www.hindawi.com/journals/aurt/2011/681627.

I'm Determined!, www.imdetermined.org.

Indiana Resource Center for Autism, www.iidc.indiana.edu/pages/irca.

LDadvisory.com, www.ldadvisory.com.

"Starting Points for Understanding Autism; Monotropism in Practice." *Medium: Psychology*, 19 Jan. 2019, www.medium.com/@Oolong/starting-points-for-understanding-autism-3573817402f2.

"Autism." *National Alliance on Mental Illness*, www.nami.org/learn-more/mental-health-conditions/autism.

"Social interaction for children." *National Autistic Society*, 21 Jul. 2017, www.autism.org.uk/about/communication/social-children.aspx.

"Autism Spectrum Disorder." *National Institute of Mental Health*,

www.nimh.nih.gov/health/topics/autism-spectrum-disorders-asd/
index.shtml.

"Autism Spectrum Disorder Fact Sheet." *National Institute of Neurological Disorders and Stroke*, www.ninds.nih.
gov/Disorders/Patient-Caregiver-Education/Fact-Sheets/
Autism-Spectrum-Disorder-Fact-Sheet.

NeuroClastic (formerly The Aspergian, A Collective of Autistic Voices),
www.neuroclastic.com.

Lynch, C.L. ""It's a Spectrum" Doesn't Mean What You Think."
*NeuroClastic (formerly The Aspergian, A Collective of Autistic
Voices)*, 4 May 2019, www.neuroclastic.com/2019/05/04/
its-a-spectrum-doesnt-mean-what-you-think.

McCrae, Mike. "People With Autism Have More Symmetrical Brains.
Here's What That Could Mean." *Science Alert*, 3 Nov. 2019, www.
sciencealert.com/people-with-autism-have-more-symmetrical-
brains-here-s-what-that-could-mean.

Leigh, Karen. "What are Pragmatic Language Skills?" *Sensational Kids,
Realizing Potential Together*, 3 Mar. 2018, www.sensationalkids.ie/
what-are-pragmatic-language-skills.

SPARK: Simons Foundation Powering Autism Research for Knowledge,
www.sparkforautism.org/portal/page/autism-research.

Deweerdt, Sarah. "Talking sense: What sensory processing disorder says about autism." *Spectrum News*, 1 Jun.
2016, www.spectrumnews.org/features/deep-dive/
talking-sense-what-sensory-processing-disorder-says-about-autism.

Luterman, Sara. "Call for help: We need to address suicide risk in autistic women." *Spectrum News*, 12 Mar.
2019, www.spectrumnews.org/opinion/viewpoint/
call-help-need-address-suicide-risk-autistic-women.

"Elizabeth Torres on Autistic Neuromotor Differences: The TPGA
Interview." *Thinking Person's Guide to Autism*, 31 Jan. 2019, www.
thinkingautismguide.com/2019/01/elizabeth-torres-on-autistic-
neuromotor.html.

"Autism Information." *U.S. Department of Health & Human Services,* www.hhs.gov/programs/topic-sites/autism/index.html.

Rudy, Lisa Jo. "Repetitive Behaviors in Autism." *Verywell Health,* 6 Oct. 2019, www.verywellhealth.com/repetitive-behaviors-in-autism-260582.

Watson Institute, www.thewatsoninstitute.org.

Would you mind leaving a few words about this book in a review at your favorite online retailer? The review can be short or long, detailed or general in nature - your opinion matters. This helps other readers decide if my book might be valuable to them.

Thanks, I do appreciate it.

If you are interested in following me or this book, my website is vivianlumbard.com. You can also find links to various social media accounts there.

Vivian

VIVIAN M. LUMBARD
AUTHOR

Made in the USA
Monee, IL
28 April 2021